T0305638

Traveling Expertise and Regional Development

This book analyses an increasingly important phenomenon in contemporary regional development, namely 'traveling expertise' and policy ideas.

Drawing on the fields of urban and regional development, and informed by the emerging school of governmentality studies, it offers a theoretically and empirically original exploration of this subject, and of the linkages between local and global contexts and their interplay more broadly. Symbolically denoting the traveling expertise as 'hired guns', the book explores different segments of the political sphere, from policy consultants and the creative class, to the polity apparatuses in which policies are recalibrated. The book presents a unique assessment of how this external expertise impacts on regional development in terms of power, politics and governance.

Traveling Expertise and Regional Development will be a valuable resource for scholars, policymakers and advanced students interested in regional development, public management and public policy.

Andreas Öjehag-Pettersson is a Senior Lecturer in Political Science at Karlstad University, Sweden. His fields of research include globalisation, marketisation and public procurement.

Tomas Mitander is a Senior Lecturer in Political Science at Karlstad University, Sweden. His fields of research include the marketisation of public governing, regionalisation and urbanisation.

Routledge Advances in Regional Economics, Science and Policy

For more information about this series, please visit www.routledge.com/series/RAIRESP

Traveling Expertise and Regional Development

Andreas Öjehag-Pettersson and
Tomas Mitander

Routledge
Taylor & Francis Group

LONDON AND NEW YORK

First published 2020 by Routledge

2 Park Square, Milton Park, Abingdon, Oxon OX14 4RN

605 Third Avenue, New York, NY 10017

Routledge is an imprint of the Taylor & Francis Group, an informa business

First issued in paperback 2021

Publisher's Note

The publisher has gone to great lengths to ensure the quality of this reprint
but points out that some imperfections in the original copies may be apparent.

British Library Cataloguing-in-Publication Data
A catalogue record for this book is available from the British Library

Library of Congress Cataloging-in-Publication Data
A catalog record has been requested for this book

ISBN: 978-1-138-56767-2 (hbk)
ISBN: 978-1-03-217344-3 (pbk)
DOI: 10.4324/9780203705605

Typeset in Bembo
by codeMantra

Contents

Figures

Acknowledgements

First of all, we would like to extend our most sincere gratitude to Line Säll who has been instrumental for the realization of this book. Her work has been, and continues to be, an inspiration for us and the research environment of which we are a part. More specifically we would also like to point out her direct contributions to the present volume as she was a part of the project early on. As such, this book started as a joint endeavor where we planned to draw on each other's knowledge, data and the work that we have carried out together before. Thus, Line helped draft the original synopsis and she also co-authored two early draft papers that we presented at conferences. Both of these were later developed, rewritten and broken up into parts of this final product, and while Line did not write the text that can be found here, she was part of the creative process that ultimately led to this book.

We would also like to thank the department of political, historical, religious and cultural studies as well as the Centre for Regional Studies (CRS) at Karlstad university for generously supporting this project. In this circumstance we would especially like to mention the continuous and always stimulating support coming from working closely together with Malin Rönnblom, David Scott and David Olsson. Thank you!

1 Introduction

Hired guns

In his 1977 book *Six Guns and Society: A Structural Study of the Western*, Will Wright pointed out how the extremely influential western genre in books, movies, and TV shows followed a certain trope or story arch through which a number of social practices and discourses were articulated. In particular, western stories very often follow the trials and tribulations of specific towns or regions that are struggling to be prosperous. Often, what stops these towns or regions from developing properly are both internal and external threats, such as corrupt legal officers, hostile 'Indian' tribes, and perhaps also some unscrupulous political elite in cahoots with insidious 'big business.'

Then, along comes the gunslinger. The lone gunman that travels through the town and takes up the challenges it faces by showing, through his actions, how the local population can come together and overcome their obstacles if they work together and follow a number of principles.

In this book, we pay attention to what we understand as new forms of such gunslingers, namely what we call *traveling expertise*. We argue that, as a phenomenon, traveling expertise has grown in importance over the last decades following what is often described as a range of important transformations across social systems in Europe and beyond. Perhaps, claims of such shifts, alterations, and 'new eras' have become somewhat of a cliché, yet it is hard to think that, for instance, the fundamental changes of state bureaucracy under the moniker New Public Management (NPM); the reconfigurations of economic and social life associated with the concepts of neoliberalism and globalization; the evolution of information technology and the internet; the end of the Cold War and the expansion of the European Union (EU) as well as the emergence of other scales and spaces of politics would not have a significant impact on what it means to govern. Of particular interest to us among these broad changes are the rise of what some have called the competition state (eg. Cerny, 1997) and new forms of regional development politics in line with so called New Regionalism (Keating, 1998). Together, we argue, these developments have helped facilitate a situation where regional policy makers find themselves in need of policies and models that help their regions succeed in a global race for talent, resources, and investments. In this context, *expertise* has become very important.

In our conception then, traveling expertise denotes an assemblage of discourses, subjects, and objects which all come together as a multiplicity of mobile articulations of how to develop regions and cities in present day. In large metropolitan areas as well as peripheral regions in the outskirts of Europe, traveling expertise ties local policy-makers together with private consultants, academic experts, and discourses of innovation, entrepreneurship, and creativity in a perpetual struggle to boost regional competitiveness. In this trope, as traveling expertise enters local sites, it provides a setting, and a script, for how cities and regions can, and should, behave in relation to the external and internal threats that disrupt and impede their development. Today such threats are represented as globalization and intense competition, and the traveling expertise, embodied in consultants and policy experts, assume the function of the lone gunmen, serving as hired guns ready to act and rally regional politics and policy around a common goal: to become globally competitive.

Here, we aim to study how this traveling expertise have effects in terms of governing as expressed in the context of regional development in Europe. To make sense of this relationship that we perceive to be fluid and non-linear in character we turn to two overlapping bodies of literature for inspiration. First, we draw on the Foucauldian notion of *governmentality* and the literature that during the last decade or so has developed this line of thinking into an increasingly important perspective within social sciences (eg. Bacchi & Goodwin, 2016; Dean, 2010; Foucault, 2007, 2008; Miller & Rose, 2008; Walters, 2012). We argue, along with others (eg. Walters, 2012:38), that as an analytics of power, governmentality is 'particularly well equipped for the analysis of contemporary liberal societies in which the governance of our health, wealth, happiness etc., is in no way the monopoly of the state and its policies.' Second, we turn to what has been called *assemblage thinking* (eg. Acuto & Curtis, 2013; Delanda, 2016; Deleuze & Guattari, 2004, 2009; Ong & Collier, 2005) where scholars have suggested certain ways of framing the objects of study, which emphasize their complex, mobile, and heterogeneous coming together into *assemblages* consisting of disparate parts.

Following these literatures, we use this first introductory chapter to flesh out our analytical points of departure in some detail in order to present the rationale for the rest of the book. We begin with asking more generally what it means to govern any aspect of social reality and then more specifically tie this together with our notion of expertise and how assemblage thinking helps us grasp the intersections of regional development and traveling expertise. Together these two sections provide us with a conceptual grammar, or a toolbox for analysis, as we position analytical categories and concepts in relation to each other and show how they can be mobilized for empirical analysis.

Thus, in the final part of this introduction we explicitly draw on this toolbox to showcase the road that lies ahead in the rest of the book. Briefly, this road is marked out by our investigation of three related moments where traveling expertise intersect and interchange with regional development. First we follow how it gives rise to (and is itself shaped by) specific *problematizations and rationalities* of governing, and second how these are nested in a relay system of *governmental technologies* that sustains them and realizes them. Third, we turn our attention to how different *subjects and subjectivities* emerge as important in relation to traveling expertise. We argue that these three moments together enable us to consider broader governmental effects in regional governance pertaining to the influence of traveling expertise. While this last section of the introduction represents a disposition for the book as such, we also like to think of it as a way for us to present the cases and the material that unfold over the following chapters as well as how we analytically tie them together through the conceptual grammar that we fashioned first.

Governing contemporary regional development

In order to show how traveling expertise affects the governing of regional development today, we must first spell out precisely what we mean by the term 'to govern.' As mentioned briefly, we do not reserve this notion for the activities of formal legislative bodies of specific institutional functions within societies. Rather, we follow a discussion that has taken place over the last three decades as scholars from many different disciplines have advanced, reinterpreted, and debated what it means 'to govern' based on a number of lectures given by Michel Foucault (2007, 2008) in the late 1970s. In these lectures Foucault stresses how a vital part of understanding the evolution of different regimes of government concerns the functions and effects of what can be called the *mentalities* nested in the art of government. Such mentalities incorporate fundamental assumptions of what it means to govern any aspect of reality and, indeed, what such a reality must be like in order for it to be governable in the first place.

While important, this line of thinking concerning governmentality is not particularly straightforward in the lectures by Foucault. Rather, governmentality as a theme, or topic, is dispersed in various circumstances and the term is used with some degree of ambiguity. Nevertheless, over the decades, scholars working with the concepts and propositions made by Foucault have helped established a school of thought that is sometimes denoted as governmentality studies (Walters, 2012). This heterodox school is now quite distinct in its development from its origins in the articulations by Foucault, and it offers an analytical register that is the result of scholars interpreting and forwarding the points made in his lectures and developing them into a form of perspective on the practice of government.

In this regard, the bulk of literature on governmentality recognizes a number of similar themes and utilizes a fairly coherent set of analytical concepts in order to describe and analyze the empirical phenomenon they are interested in. That being said, we do not consider governmentality studies to provide a theory in a strong sense of the word. Rather, we follow William

Walters (2012:459) in his suggestion that we can use the rather extensive body of work that draws on governmentality as inspiration or 'as something to be used, adapted [and] set to work in grappling with problems.' In short, we argue that the governmentality perspective offers a toolbox from which we can draw a set of components that can help us analyze and make sense of traveling expertise and its relationship with the governing of regional development. More precisely, by paying attention to how governing is understood to be nested in *problematizations*, how these, in turn, are connected to certain *political rationalities* and *governmental technologies*, as well as how these help produce *subjects and objects*, we will illustrate how traveling expertise is reproduced within regional development. Therefore, below we specify how Foucault's legacy, as articulated through governmentality studies, helps us in this regard.

Governmentality studies

It is common to contrast two different (but related) meanings that Foucault (1991, 2007, 2008) attributed to the term *governmentality* in his lectures at *Collège de France* during the late 1970s and early 1980s. First, during the course of these lectures he addresses what he finds to be a specific development of state rule that took place during late modernity. As such, this process was related to the emergence of liberal states and the changing focus for the governing apparatus at that time. According to Foucault (2007), the focus for state rule around this time shifted so that it now became explicitly concerned with the wellbeing of its population or, as he would call it, its biopolitics. This was related to new forms of power as sovereignty and discipline was no longer as clearly connected to a single ruling monarch. Instead, the population within a certain territory now became one of its most vital resources that could be optimized and utilized in particular ways. Over time then, states started to enclose their populations within different forms of security systems such as the police, the military, diplomatic forces, education, health care, and welfare. Foucault (2007) shows how this also means that the state had to enter a new order of reason where economy and economic rationale were to become very central. In this *neoliberalism*, it was not only a matter of making room for a market logic, rather, the state was to be transformed:

> I tried to show you how the problem of neo-liberalism was not how to cut out or contrive a free space of the market within an already given political society, as in the liberalism of Adam Smith and the eighteenth century. The problem of neo-liberalism is rather how the overall exercise of political power can be modeled on the principles of a market economy. So it is not a question of freeing an empty space, but taking the formal principles of a market economy and referring and relating them to, of projecting them on to a general art of government.
>
> (Foucault, 2007:131)

Thus, the first meaning of governmentality can be understood as this particular manifestation of a form of government that rules its population primarily through its economic registers and tries to foster its populations into subjects that can be utilized in different ways.

In the second sense of the word, governmentality must be interpreted more generally than as one or many instances of historically located regimes of rule. Rather, it denotes how *to govern* is a practice nested in discursively produced mentalities or forms of thinking and ways of representing truth. In this regard, Foucault (1991, 2007, 2008) invites us to consider what it means to govern in the first place, and what conditions of possibility that enables it. He then begins with noting that we may think of government as the 'conduct of conduct.' This wordplay emphasizes that governing is an activity that strives to steer, control or order (conduct as a verb) the behavior, composure or acting (conduct as a noun) of something or someone (Foucault, 2007:191ff). Importantly, this means that to govern is not an activity exclusively reserved for what we traditionally call the government or the formal political apparatus in a society. Rather, governing takes place in many different forms and involves a range of actors not affiliated with formal or official political power. Indeed, governing in this sense is also exercised at the level of the self.

Since governing is not an exclusive matter for the state, from a governmentality perspective various forms of expertise may be involved in the governing (conduct of conduct) of any given domain of reality. In order to grasp these various forms of power that attempts to steer, guide or control, governmentality studies are often interested in fields or domains as the surfaces where governing takes place. Thus, the sick, the healthy, the ecology, the economy, the penal system, and the elderly are all examples of domains that have become the objects of government. These domains are referred to with different terms such as regimes of practice, assemblages of rule, dispositifs or apparatuses. While the terms actually have different conceptual connotations, they generally signify that any object of rule is a complex arrangement of discourses, subjects, and objects that are brought together in a somewhat stable, yet never complete, affiliation.

Thus, governmentality, in this sense, is a form of analysis directed towards precisely the *mentalities* of government, and it is interested in how certain domains of reality become the object of rule and how they become the target of programmatic thought that renders them amenable for intervention. Following anthropologist Tania Murray Li (2007), we argue that an important first step in this process can be called the moment of problematization and rendering technical.

Problematizations and rendering technical

In Foucauldian thought, and more specifically in governmentality studies, the notion of 'problematization' is a central feature (cf. Bacchi, 2012). While its precise meaning may vary somewhat depending on author and circumstance,

from a governmentality perspective it generally involves the position that political problems are not external to the act of governing. Rather, an important
moment in governing any domain or element of reality involves pinpointing
it in terms of a problem that may be corrected with a certain set of prescribed
measures. Thus, problems do not merrily sit there out in the world, waiting
to be corrected, rather, as put by Miller and Rose (2008:15) 'if a particular
diagnosis or tool appears to fit a particular "problem," this is because they
have been made so that they fit each other.'

Therefore, scholars may follow and analyze the way that particular representations of a problem become part of governing and how, in this sense,
we are governed through problematizations (eg. Bacchi, 2009, 2012). Since
this process is intrinsic to rule, another point is that there are no neutral
positions here. To govern is political, although often the moment of problematization conceals this dimension by mobilizing power in such ways
that alternative representations of a problem are pushed aside (Murray Li,
2007). Here, the mentalities of rule become important in a very fundamental sense. The ways we represent problems as the object of governing are
nested in particular forms of knowledge and claims for truth (c.f Bacchi,
2009), and therefore, studying problem representations may help identi-
fying the ideological regimes at play in this particular formulation of the
problem.

To illustrate this fundamental point that problem representations, rather
than 'objectively' existing problems, are the bases for governing, consider
one of the several examples provided by Bacchi (2009). Suppose a government in a given society identifies that children are obese to an extent that
is found to be problematic and therefore launches various activity programs
directed towards the children with the intention of getting them to move
more. Now, this way of representing the problem could have been made
quite differently. In this case, the way the problem is constituted is that it is
actually a matter of children's inactivity. It doesn't take long to come up with
a number of different 'solutions' to the problem of obesity, which are based
in different representations of the problem. For instance, if the government
instead would have deployed a ban on fast food commercials, the problem
of obesity would have been represented as having something to do with the
capitalist economy and marketing products to children. Thus, governmentality scholars stress the importance of this process where government makes
problems in close connection with the deployment of policies that aim to
rectify them. In short, the attention to this is argued to provide insights into
the prevailing rationalities and discourses that make up the conditions of
possibility for governing (Bacchi & Goodwin, 2016; Dean, 2010; Miller &
Rose, 2008).

Furthermore, for scholars working from a governmentality perspective,
this moment of problematization is also crucially interlinked with a moment
of 'rendering technical' (Murray Li, 2007). This means that as a problem is
made, it must be constituted in such ways that it is possible to act upon by the

government, so that policies can be directed towards it and measures taken so as to ensure the success of governing in one direction or another. This may sound simple, but often requires significant governmental effort in itself. Not least, it usually involves the coordination, selection, and promotion of various forms of expertise that can help constitute the problem at hand and, in this way, make it governable.

Finally, the constitutions of problems and their link to a moment of rendering technical also illustrates another principal point made by many governmentality scholars, namely that governing as an activity can be called *programmatic*. As put by Miller and Rose (2008:29) to understand governing as programmatic helps draw attention not only to how it operates though programs to conduct the conduct of various problems, but also to how governing at its core rests on the assumption that reality is steerable, controllable – or, in short, programmable:

> Governmentality is programmatic not simply in that one can see the proliferation of more or less explicit programmes for reforming reality – government reports, White Papers, Green Papers, papers from business, trade unions, financiers, political parties, charities and academics proposing this or that scheme for dealing with this or that problem. It is also programmatic in that it is characterized by an eternal optimism that a domain or society could be administered better or more effectively, that reality is, in some way or other, programmable.
>
> (Miller & Rose, 2008:29)

Thus, we find it important to keep in mind that governing any domain of social reality always rests on a certain will to program that reality in accordance with the ideals of structuring discourses and rationalities. In sum then, in studies of governmentality, it is common to highlight how governing is an activity nested in specific ways of representing problems, which also rests on a basic assumption concerning the programmatic character of reality in the first place. This is a point of departure for understanding the fundamentals of governing any domain, and before moving on to other aspects of how governing is enacted, the analytical importance of understanding the representation and constitution of problems should not be underestimated.

Political rationalities and governmental technologies

Another common theme in the governmentality literature concerns how governing is enacted as policies are put to work and made operational in relation to a particular problematization. Two main analytical categories are often discussed to understand this process, namely *political rationalities* and *governmental technologies*. These are closely linked; however, neither one is reducible to the other. First, the political rationalities can be understood as the underlying, internal logic that must be in place in order to problematize a given domain in a particular way and not another. In other words, as we govern we are guided by these political rationalities that make certain pre-suppositions and assumptions logical as well as make the separate steps of policy programs designed to address the identified problem seem reasonable. Importantly, this is not 'just' a matter of bias in terms of party politics but a question of more fundamental nature in the sense that the rationalities rest upon specific ontological and epistemological assumptions, which enables certain forms of governing, while circumventing others.

Another way of expressing the function of political rationalities can be to think of them as the underlying logic for a particular way of governing. In other words, to make them visible scholars may ask 'what forms of thought, knowledge, expertise, strategies [and] means of calculation' (Dean, 2010:42) are nested in the ways that rule is articulated? Thus, according to Bacchi and Goodwin (2016:42) political rationalities are 'the rationales produced to jus-tify particular modes of rule' and they function as ways that make any form of activity thinkable to both rulers and the ruled. These diagrams of power 'draw upon the theories, ideas, philosophies, and forms of knowledge that characterize our intellectual heritage,' (Bacchi & Goodwin, 2016:43) which means that most contemporary policy making in liberal states involve the social and human sciences quite extensively.

Second, as for governmental technologies, they represent, in this per-spective, the means through which rationalities can be rolled out. By ask-ing through what 'mechanisms, procedures, instruments, tactics, techniques, technologies, and vocabularies is authority constituted and rule accomplished' (Dean, 2010:42) governmentality studies have shed light on how mundane apparatuses such as a form to fill out at a government agency as well as spec-tacular arrangements such as benchmarking conferences for regions, fill an important and specific function in rendering the problem at hand technical, and thus to enable rule according to whatever political rationalities that are involved. Moreover, it is important to keep in mind that the governmental technologies are not reduced to a second class category that merely serves as an infrastructure for the political rationalities, but rather governmentality studies emphasize how technologies of rule also form rationalities and affect the way we think of a problem.

Another way to put it then is that as a domain is being made the object of governing the governmental technologies are what enable rule. They are forms of interventions that are made so as to, alluding to the works of Bruno Latour (eg. 1987), make 'governing at a distance' possible. They are then a form of relay system that is capable of putting rationalities and programmes into motion as well as providing feedback to the rulers about the ruled. For example, consider how governing regions today is a practice full of statistical surveys, measurement tools for gauging and counting the performance con-cerning a wide array of functions, project plans and forms to fill out for fund-ing applications from certain agencies, as well as formal principles for guiding partnerships between public and private bodies. Such tools are understood here to be important and intrinsic technologies of government, deployed in order to configure certain domains of the social into governable spaces. And again, to repeat an important point, we understand these instruments not only as expressions of, but also as active parts in producing, certain political rationalities (Dean, 2010; Miller & Rose, 2008).

Subjects of rule

Finally then, as a third important theme in governmentality studies, one can point to how this school of thought generally understands the subjects of rule. Rather than following what, perhaps, is a more mainstream understanding of humans as rational actors with a more or less essential set of preferences and attributes, governmentality scholars pay attention to what they understand as processes of subjectification. This means that there is no assumption of an essential trait in human beings with regards to the desires, dreams, and actions that govern their behavior in different circumstances. Instead such dispositions are thought to emerge as effects of power where we as humans inhabit a range of possible subject positions at the same time. Certainly, this way of thinking about actors and subjects in the social sciences is not exclusive to governmentality research. Rather, it is part of a wider post-structuralist tradition of reasoning (Glynos & Howarth, 2007; Howarth, 2013) in various forms of discourse analysis (eg. Jörgensen & Philips, 2002; Laclau & Mouffe, 2001; Wodak & Meyer, 2009), in psychoanalysis (eg. Lacan, 2018), in feminist perspectives (eg. Butler, 1993) as well as in post-humanist perspectives (Barad, 2007). While this is not the place to develop all the important interventions in theories of the subject (cf. Mansfield, 2000), it is important to recognize that for governmentality scholars, the ideas of subjectification and subjectivities are closely related to the act of governing and the 'repertoires of conduct' that are made available to different subjects through governing and policy (Bacchi & Goodwin, 2016:49). Thus, following Dean (2010:43) we can state that an important focus for governmentality studies is their 'attention to the formation of identities.' This means that scholars working from this perspective generally are interested in how political rationalities and governmental technologies are complacent in the formulation of (un)desired subjects, and indeed, how they presuppose certain ideas of the subjects that are to be governed:

> We might ask in relation to this final axis: what forms of person, self and identity are presupposed by different perspectives of government and what sorts of transformation do these practices seek? What statuses, capacities, attributes and orientations are assumed of those who exercise authority (from politicians and bureaucrats to professionals and therapists) and those who are to be governed (workers, consumers, pupils and social welfare recipients)? What forms of conduct are expected of them?
>
> (Dean, 2010:43)

This position then views the ruled subject not as the starting point for an analysis of governing, but rather as an effect of it. This means that the subject is the vehicle of governing programmes rather than a bastion of resistance that exists beyond any regimes of power that operate as governing is enacted. Indeed, in various places throughout his publications and lectures Foucault spoke of the subject as his primary interest, something that in a way ties together his different theoretical endeavors. While his expressions concerning this matter vary, they generally revolve around making the point that the subject is an effect of power:

> The individual is not conceived as a sort of elementary nucleus, a primitive atom, a multiple and inert material on which power comes to fasten or against which it happens to strike, and in so doing subdues or crushes individuals. In fact, it is already one of the prime effects of power that certain bodies, certain gestures, certain discourses, certain desires, come to be identified and constituted as individuals. The individual, that is, is not the vis-à-vis of power; it is, I believe, one of its prime effects. The individual is an effect of power, and at the same time, or precisely to the extent which it is that effect, it is the element of its articulation. The individual which power has constituted is at the same time its vehicle.
>
> (Foucault, 1980:98)

At the same time, this certainly does not mean that we as subjects are never able to resist governance practices or that we are reducible to the results of planned and calculated acts of governing. It does, however, mean that an important part of governing any domain of social reality includes promoting, eliciting, and facilitating various identities and subject positions for the ruled. We argue that an attention to such aspects allows for important insights into the political dimensions of all governing in at least two ways.

First, by focusing on the construction of governable subjects in policy and governing it is possible to observe what Bacchi and Goodwin (2016) call 'dividing practices.' Dividing practices work through dynamic ways of differentiation and subordination in governing where oppositional and binary groups are often positioned explicitly or implicitly against each other in policy. So for instance, as practices of governing are set into motion, they may demarcate and distinguish between such binaries as 'citizen/migrant, youth/adult, responsible/irresponsible, man/woman, disabled/fit, welfare recipient/tax payer, etc.' (Bacchi & Goodwin, 2016:51).

Second, the construction of governable subjects also shows the political dimension in the ways that humans readily construct themselves as subjects through the acts of governing. Indeed, to become a legitimate subject within a given policy field humans, more or less, must reconstruct themselves in accordance with the positions made available to them by governing. In a sense, to be able to address power and to make ourselves present in governing we need to speak on its terms. In short, in certain situations we can only be entrepreneurs or workers, and we must construct ourselves around those subject positions to be able exist at all in such situations.

In sum then, we follow governmentality studies and their focus on the governable subject as a result of power and governing rather than a starting point. It means that instead of assuming the existence of certain actors that are important as traveling expertise intermesh with regional development and starting out by asking questions such as 'what kind of actions are taken by this or that actor?' or 'which actor is most powerful here?' we follow a different route. Our analyses and observations do not presuppose actors or individuals and our questions are laid out along the lines of 'who was conceived of as an actor here?,' 'in what circumstances?,' and 'with what capacities?' (Jäger & Maier, 2009).

Assemblage thinking

So far we have spoken about governmentality studies as a strand of literature that we draw on for inspiration when we aim to make sense of governing effects associated with traveling expertise in regional development. While we argue that this provides us with a set of analytical concepts and positions that allows us to frame our idea of what governing means and how it can be approached systematically, we now turn our interest towards how we conceptualize the notion of traveling expertise. In order to do so we pick up on some of the most influential works that use the figure of an *assemblage* as a way of delineating cases, theorize objects, and analyze material. To reiterate then, at an abstract level we understand the assemblage of traveling expertise to be a contingent amalgamation of certain discourses, practices, and subjects that together form a specific set of relations that can be approached empirically. Before moving further, we wish to situate this conception with respect to other work with similar approaches, and more specifically we wish to articulate how we do *not* aspire to mobilize what some researchers have started to call assemblage theory (eg. Delanda, 2016). Instead, rather than engaging with theories of what an assemblage 'is' and how it 'really' functions, we wish to use it as a concept, or tactic for framing our study and guide or line of inquiry (Acuto & Curtis, 2013; Ong & Collier, 2005). Hence, we speak of assemblage thinking or thinking assemblages (rather than assemblage theory) as an overarching meta position that will set out structures for how to study the phenomenon we are interested in.

For us, the primary function of thinking assemblages relates to our framing of the 'objects' that we think are involved in governing processes. In short, thinking assemblages help us set the perimeters for the study at hand by providing a way of writing about abstractions such as traveling expertise or, for that matter, regional development. Our way of thinking assemblages, however, is based on the theoretical formulations made by Deleuze and

Guattari (2004, 2009). Thus, we start our conceptions in their definitions of an assemblage. An often reproduced quote by Deleuze presents this definition as:

> What is an assemblage? It is a multiplicity which is made up of heterogeneous terms… the assemblage's only unity is that of co-functioning: it is a symbiosis, a 'sympathy.' It is never filiations that are important, but alliances, alloys.
>
> (Deleuze & Parnet, 2007:69)

For us, this means that to think assemblages is to focus on the intersections where the multiplicities meet and form. In more concrete terms, when we say that we approach the phenomenon of traveling expertise as an assemblage, we denote how such expertise is a coming together of a range of disparate components such as policies for how to do something, research on relevant topics, the performances of policy gurus, conferences, benchmarking instruments, websites, breakfast meetings as well as the technical infrastructure needed to fit such parts together.

Thus, in general terms, an assemblage lays out a grid of relations among component parts and fits them together. In doing so, however, it is more like a machine than an organic whole or unity. The assemblage is solely defined by its external relations and, therefore, it is not 'a thing' as such. Moreover, the elements of the assemblage are not pieces of a jigsaw puzzle that fit in specific ways and only in those specific ways. Rather, the machine qualities of an assemblage is precisely that it enables combinations, mixtures, and recombinations of external fragments, or what Deleuze and Guattari (2009) call 'singularities.' Hence, it makes no sense to call out for the essence of a given assemblage. It is never really a finished or a complete product. Therefore, when studying an assemblage we do not ask 'what is… X or Y.' Rather we ask, 'how do X manifest,' 'where and when are X and Y combined,' or 'from what view point does Y emerge.' At an abstract level, therefore, assemblage thinking enables studies of events rather than essences and unities.

In terms of traveling expertise, therefore, we do not start here by giving it an essentialist definition by listing a specific set of qualities that must be in place for us to speak of it. Instead, for us, traveling expertise in regional development is an assemblage in the sense described above – a grid of relations that pulls together various elements and positions them in specific ways. Similar to how Newman and Clark (2009:9) describe how they draw on assemblage thinking to approach 'publicness,' for us 'the idea of assemblage points to the ways in which policies, personnel, places, practices, technologies, images, architectures of governance, and resources are brought together and combined' with respect to expertise. This means that we study a material and a circumstance where expertise is produced as a vital part of governing regional development. In more tangible terms this may mean, for instance, that we explicitly draw on material such as reports written by subjects of expertise, or it means that we show how, in the context of governing regional development, expertise emerges as vital.

Thinking assemblages this way, in a certain sense, points us to the issues before method, to the ways of framing our inquiry. In the present study, we use it as a way to make sense of a very large set of data, accumulated over the course of the past ten years in various studies concerning the governing of regional development in Europe with a special focus on the Nordic. In this data, what we have seen is precisely a set of relations that ties elements together through what we have labeled traveling expertise. We call it traveling, as we recognize how some of the most significant aspects of this assemblage is precisely its mobile quality. The expertise involved in regional development is produced in ways that make it readily available in a vast range of contexts throughout Europe and beyond. Moreover, it has effects that are similar in terms of governing. That being said, at an abstract level we maintain that it is still important to recognize that while assemblages often have mobile and even global aspects (Ong & Collier, 2005), they do mutate and change with the local context in which they are inserted. Indeed, one can argue that this ability to translate elements of expertise so that they fit into different circumstances is what gives this assemblage one of its most vital qualities – the ability to travel.

Putting it all together: the road from here

So far we have been detailing our points of departure in terms of theoretical inspiration and positioning. We have said that we approach traveling expertise in regional development as an assemblage and that as such we are primarily interested in how this is governed. More specifically, leaning on the literature of governmentality, we argue that traveling expertise is both an effect of governing while at the same time also producing effects by itself. We are therefore interested in the political rationalities that enable the assemblage of traveling expertise to exist in the first place as well as in how these rationalities are shaped by the same expertise. Similarly, we argue that it is equally important to understand the governmental technologies that sustain and relay the rationalities throughout the assemblage. Finally, we also wish to turn our attention to the subjectivities that are produced as part of the assemblage. This rather basic three part structure is also the way we have chosen to present the rest of the book. Before moving on to the disposition, however, we wish to specify a bit more in detail what data we draw on and what kind of analysis we argue for in the following parts of the book.

About the cases and data

We have spent the past decade studying regional development in Europe with a specific focus on Sweden and the Nordic countries. For us, this book is a way to communicate the findings drawn from different research projects and to connect different sources of data and empirical sites. Thus, we draw on large datasets generated as part of multiple five year research projects directed towards broad questions such as the issues of citizenship and globalization in contemporary regional development. In addition, we also draw on data generated as part of shorter research projects during this time where we have studied, among other things, gender equality struggles in regional development, the role of consultants and consultancy in public administration (with a specific focus on regional development) as well as the production of benchmarking tools and rankings that allow for different measurements and comparisons among regions. Moreover, since 2010 we have been involved with, and currently direct, a recurring large scale survey in which a representative sample of citizens in a Swedish region answer questions concerning, among other things, regional development.

This means that in the following we base our presentation on interviews, focus groups, document studies, media reports, observations, participations, and several waves of large surveys. As mentioned, they span over the last decade and include views and positions from politicians, civil servants, citizens, and a wide range of experts such as academics and consultants. In other words, we feel confident that this data can be used to detail, describe, and theorize the important facets of regional development today. That being said, the purpose of this book is not to present all details of this data, but rather to utilize it and illustrate what we identify as the effects of governing pertaining to the assemblage of traveling expertise in regional development. Inevitably, this means that we will present arguments and make claims that are at a rather abstract, or perhaps theoretical, level with respect to the data. For the sake of this kind of argumentation and empirical analysis, we find it important to spell out some of its details. In particular, we want to detail some of our thoughts concerning empirical illustrations as part of our analysis and how we may think about what we present here in terms of case logics.

Empirical illustrations, analysis, and paradigmatic case logic

First off, in the coming chapters of this book we utilize what we label *empirical illustrations*. For us, this means that we do not intend to make the material as a whole 'justice.' As mentioned, it has been generated with different purposes in mind, yet it also fits together and is usable to illustrate the assemblage of traveling expertise in regional development. This allows us to present an analysis where the material is used to illuminate particular facets of political rationalities, governmental technologies, and subjectivities that are important for understanding the workings of traveling expertise. As such, we draw on our data here to illustrate what we find to be salient themes and topics in terms of political rationalities, governmental technologies, and subjectivities. However, it is worth emphasizing that the approach taken here does not exhaust the data. Rather, by salient themes and topics we mean such aspects of the data that in many ways structure it and are of central concern for understanding the material as a whole. Again, this data spans over a decade and has been generated with different (yet related) purposes in mind. This means, for instance, that we do not detail the different processes of data generation more than what we simply mention here, and we are not particularly concerned with showing the differences and nuances that naturally exist between the cases from which data is drawn. Rather, we aim to treat this data together as one set and fashion what we consider a *paradigmatic case* for regional development in Europe (at least).

Paradigmatic cases, according to Flyvbjerg (2006), convey one out of four major varieties of case selection logics upon which researchers can draw valid conclusions. Paradigmatic cases are utilized to showcase what may be considered 'more general characteristics of the societies in question' (Flyvbjerg, 2006:232), and this is achieved by constructing exemplars or prototypes of general tendencies that are valid in broader settings. The way that we draw on our data here is along such lines. Our ambition is to portray the field of regional development, not in one country or context, but rather throughout the contemporary field as such. When doing so we use metaphors and abstractions that we argue can be placed alongside any actually existing case in a given country and thereby enable a reading of that particular case that is based on the general tendencies of the field.

To sum up, in the three analytical chapters of this book, we utilize these empirical illustrations together with the governmentality approach to make general points and to showcase broader tendencies. We start each chapter by providing a vignette which is a fictionalized example drawn from our own experiences researching the field. We want these vignettes to give a sense of these broader tendencies, and then we try to stick with it during the chapter as we work with the data. Each chapter is then summed up in a way that draws together the points made by relating them to the notion of traveling expertise. This allows us to continuously make general claims for how the governing of regional development is marked by the notion of expertise. A final caveat may be needed with respect to the fact that even though we treat the data in the way we discuss here, and while we are not trying to make empirical generalizations, we are mostly situated in an EU context, and even more specifically our primary experience is with regional development of Nordic countries, particularly Sweden.

Disposition

Following this first introductory chapter we present our study over three main chapters. Before that, however, we wish to situate the book in its empirical context of regional development. Hence, in Chapter 2 we account for what we call a 'grand narrative' of regional development. Naturally, this presentation sketches major themes and developments rather than being very detailed. The intention is, however, to present the 'common knowledge,' or discursive backdrop, within the policy field and the scholarly field of regional development.

In Chapter 3 we turn to the political rationalities of contemporary regional development as we detail what we identify as a master rationality of competitiveness that guides and steers the governing of this practice. Paying attention to the fact that a lot of rhetoric in regional development draws on militaristic references we then use metaphors consistent with this as we tease out three political rationalities that we argue operate as intertwined with the master one. Thus, by describing first *the rationality of the strategos*, then *the rationality of triage* and finally *the rationality of intelligence*, we highlight how regional development today is a very fertile ground for the spawning of traveling expertise, and in many direct examples it is the product of said expertise.

In Chapter 4 we turn to governmental technologies that help sustain and relay traveling expertise in the field of regional development. We focus on two such technologies that we aim to present broadly by not only illustrating them empirically but also by contextualizing them theoretically. First, we describe the technology of quantification, ranking, and indexing, or even more broadly speaking, various techniques and practices utilized to facilitate benchmarking. Second, we show how techniques of multimodality are prevalent features of most policy documentation in the field. By this we mean that a lot of the official publications produced resemble marketing brochures for business rather than more 'plain' policy publications. By examining how they are filled with imagery, typography, and graphic design we lay bare certain effects of power that we later discuss in terms of traveling expertise.

In Chapter 5, the last of the three analytical chapters, we examine the processes of subjectification and show the production of subjects of expertise. Here, we detail the representations of five social actors and how they are produced in the assemblage of traveling expertise as it merges with regional development. Thus, the region, the corporation, the women, the immigrants, and the experts are presented and exemplified before we provide an explicit discussion concerning their relationship with expertise.

Finally, in Chapter 6, we provide a discussion of what we have shown in the book as we argue that traveling expertise is intimately connected to processes of depoliticization. Indeed, we argue that in present day regional development there is a tendency to reproduce what we label a post-polis, a political community that has evolved beyond conventional connotations of liberal democracy in some quite bothersome ways.

2 Transitions in regional development and the role of expertise

> The single most important question is going to be if the region has the ability to maintain and increase its competitiveness.
>
> $(01)^1$

There are some simple truths about regional development. Some statements that can be made without the risk of being challenged or frowned upon, even by people you would consider your ideological adversaries. The quote above, from a regional development document in Sweden, is such a statement. It is not meant to be controversial. It is not stated as the beginning of a discussion with an intention to convince anyone. It is simply a reminder of the basic reason of contemporary regional development. The field of regional development is permeated by a *grand narrative* that has developed in a reciprocal dynamic between policy making and research during the last decades where the 'simple truths' of the core context and dynamics of contemporary regional development are formulated and consolidated (Lovering, 1999).

In this chapter our aim is to present this grand narrative; not in its totality and not with every possible nuance. Instead, we want to introduce the general contextual backdrop of how regional development is understood in contemporary time; the common sense, the simple facts, the statements that can be made without stirring up controversy among either regional policy makers or scholars of regional politics. We will do so by introducing a general shift in the grand narrative of regional development, which has characterized the past three decades, and we will describe four core aspects – or dynamics – that this shift has entailed. This grand narrative is, as we see it, absolutely crucial for understanding how the rationalities, the technologies, and the subjectivities of contemporary regional development policies are made sensible and reasonable. As the following chapters move on in their more analytically detailed work, they all do so in relation to this grand narrative, with the intention of discussing its political effects with a focus on the role of expertise.

A grand narrative

During the past decades, the paradigm of regional development has undergone some dramatic changes in Europe and beyond. There has been a major shift not only in the role of regions in development policies and the way policies should be deployed in order for regions to be effective in that role but also in the relational understanding of the spatiality of subnational regions. The way in which the perceived effects of globalization and globally mobile capital are believed to change the game of development policies has in this sense restructured the understanding of how regions matter and how they should behave in order to be successful in the strive for development and prosperity (Mitander, 2015; Mitander et al., 2013; Öjehag-Pettersson, 2015; Säll, 2014). A powerful and influential way to describe this major shift within the literature on regional development is to talk about the movement from 'old' to 'new' regionalism. In his influential book from 1998, Michael Keating described this shift from old to new regionalism – which he traces from the 1980s – as a reconfiguration of the role of regions deeply connected to the globalization of capitalism. His main argument is that the economic globalization and the global mobility of capital have transformed the territorial sovereignty of nation states in terms of an undermined capacity to regulate and control the way that international markets influence the development within the territory of the state (Keating, 1998, 2003, 2013). This development is described as leading to an increased belief that sub-national regions are more fit to act in this fast moving, elusive global terrain of capital and resources. This belief can be related to the 'hollowing out' of the nation state, where economic globalization is viewed as severely challenging the state's capacity to control, regulate, and govern its territory from an economic perspective (Rhodes, 1994). The pace, intensity, and scope of global capital mobility are understood in a way that cannot be matched by states or the development of global political institutions. In this narrative, regions find themselves in a global terrain of capital and resources, not anymore as shielded (or controlled) by the state, competing for investments and knowledge directly on international markets (cf. Fawn, 2009; Jones & MacLeod, 1999, 2004; Paasi, 2009)

The traditional regionalism is described by Keating as provincial, focused on a region–state relationship, and rendered through a nation state planning context of regional development. The new regionalism is characterized by a forward-looking, modernization-oriented, globalized understanding of the conditions and function of regions in development policy. If the regions as actors earlier had an interest to influence the national development policies from a distributional perspective, in more recent times, they operate directly on global markets, competing for resources and capital needed for development in line with the narrative of new regionalism (Keating, 1998; Loughlin, 2007; Syssner, 2006). The argument inherent in this narrative makes it clear that we are not just dealing with the case of shifting development policies, but rather, a structural pivot point where the globalization of capitalism generates new conditions and ultimately transforms the relationship between nation states, subnational regions, and the global arena.

In the following sections, we will dig deeper into this grand narrative and draw on four central aspects of it in order to illustrate how it influences and characterizes the rationales of regional development as a policy field.

From redistribution to competition

One of the most prominent features of the transforming role of the regions and the region–state relationship in this grand narrative relates to the foundational logic of how regional development comes about and which dynamics that matter for pursuing development for a region. When Keating (1998) describes the traditional regionalism as mainly focused on region–state relationships, he refers to the traditional understanding of sub-national regions as parts of a more or less centralized state system. Regions are pieces of a national puzzle, which are interlinked through processes of governing, influence, and the national dispersion of resources. These processes include how nation states govern and maintain their territorial sovereignty through regional presence, and also how democratic legitimacy for the state can be upheld through the representation of regional interests in planning processes (Keating, 1998). They also include the general notion that regional development policy is a way to maintain a basic form of equality between different geographical parts of the state, through centralized systems of redistribution and welfare services. Regions as pieces of a state puzzle is, in this traditional sense, viewed as a tool to mitigate geographical differences in living conditions and access to welfare services (Hörnström, 2010).

The structural pivot point of globalized capitalism and unregulated global flows of capital and its effects on the understanding of regions and regional development are traced by Line Säll (2014) in her study of Swedish regional development policy. In her study, she takes her empirical point of departure in the 1990s and from debates, assessments, and bills shows how the policy field of regional development was structured in three pretty much equally powerful discourses, bringing meaning to the function of sub-national regions. She calls them the rationality of distribution, the rationality of participation, and the rationality of competition. So, during the 1990s the understanding of regions was politicized in terms that the role of regions and regional development could be understood from a political equality perspective, from a centralistic, distributive state perspective, or from a global economic perspective. In her analysis of the 2000:s, Säll (2014) shows that this has dramatically changed and the rationality of competition has taken a dominant, hegemonic position in structuring the understanding of the role of regions and regional development. This transformation was made possible by the rationality of competition either pushing out alternative understandings as threats to competitiveness or through the incorporation and cooptation of alternative elements, making articulations of redistribution and democracy subordinate to the primacy of competitiveness (Säll, 2014). Her analysis can be understood as an illustration of how the new grand narrative of regional development is consolidated through a new dominating articulation of the function of the region (see also Cox, 2009; Keating, 2003; Peck, 2005).

From centralism to autonomy

The second aspect of the new regionalist narrative that we find important to highlight concerns the relationship between globalization and increased regional autonomy. Along these lines, new regionalism has been successful in promoting reforms that enhance the regional freedom to act and engage with global markets around Europe and beyond. Thus, regionalization of policy fields, a greater influence over planning processes as well as the mandate and the means to organize and act outside the territorial borders of the nation states are but some examples of this (Harrison, 2006; Hooghe et al., 2010; Mitander, 2015; Säll, 2012; Syssner, 2006). Regionalization as a structural transformation can thus be understood as a process with both domestic and international drivers and implications within the grand narrative. Within states, regions have been mandated a more autonomous role in relation to the central state to develop and implement strategies and policies for development based on particular regional conditions. Strategies such as cluster formations and smart specialization are examples of regional development strategies that emphasize the utilization of particular regional characteristics as drivers for development (Cooke, 1992; Morgan, 2007; Porter, 1990, 1998; Säll, 2014). At the same time, these strategies are often initiated and governed through international and supranational institutions. Within the European Union, the strategy to work with European integration through targeting sub-national regions has not only been a way for the EU to bypass the state level but has also resulted in institutionalized ways for regions to act globally without the mandate of the central state (Bache, 2007; Keating, 2013; Loughlin, 2007).

The new terrain of globalized capitalism as perceived in the grand narrative of regional development not only has effects on how the political world is perceived and the rationales for governing but also has very concrete institutional effects in the dispersion of authority and mandate through a restructuring of the state.

From democracy to attractiveness

The new regionalism narrative has not only changed the form and the intuitional settings for development policy but also has reshaped the logics of policy adaptation in a way that affects the very rationale for development. Earlier processes of regionalization and agenda setting in regional development have been driven by visions of subsidiarity and democratization, connected to the rationalities of distribution and participation as described by Säll (2014). Similarly, reforms have been justified through their empowering outcome, where regional citizens can come closer to political decision-making and gain influence over how national development policies are articulated. In short, an important rationale has been to move the perspectives of citizens closer to power, facilitating representation, and utilizing the democratic institutions for handling and acting out ideological conflicts. The new regionalist narrative on the other hand contends that in the era of global competition, the expectations of regionalization reforms must change since the drivers behind them are different. The reforms that are being made and argued for as necessary parts of the new regionalism narrative are not first and foremost aiming to increase the political influence for regional citizens. Instead, what regional autonomy is supposed to entail is to make the region attractive on a global market of capital and resources (Peck & Tickel, 2002). In a critical reflection on new regionalism, the British human geographer John Lovering describes this development as 'policies to replace the "imagined communities" at the national level with an "imagined unit of competition" at the local/regional level" (Lovering, 1999:392).

Attractiveness thus becomes the objective for regional development policies within the grand narrative in the sense that the way to be successful in the global competition for resources is to create reasons for those resources to be attracted to the region. To be attractive for capital investments there has to be arguments as to why returns would be higher in one particular region than in another one. Thus, if a well-managed corporation in a lucrative market is to start franchise in, or even relocate to, a given region, this region has to present its added values (availability of skilled workers, infrastructure, etc.) for the corporation to do so. Similarly, if the skilled workers are to settle down in the region there has to be the right kind of living environment for them, and so on. To put things blunt, since the 1990s, the way to be successful in governing a region towards development has been about navigating different ways to increase attractiveness for the resources that are believed to be needed (Bristow, 2005).

Innovation systems and regional leadership

The fourth aspect of the new regionalist narrative that we wish to draw on here is its emphasis on how, in the era of a knowledge economy, the main strategy to become an attractive region for global investments growth must be the focus on innovation. Generating new products, services, and business models is viewed as the way for regions and countries to be competitive when not being able to compete with low wages. Regional innovation systems are an example of a particular strategy to foster economic growth through building an infrastructure for creating innovations, in this case mostly through agglomerative strategies and through creating public–private partnerships and networks. One of its expressions is the triple helix model that has been a specific policy strategy to boost competitiveness through cooperation and specialization by coordinating between public policy makers, businesses, and academic institutions. More generally, the innovation systems promoted in the new regionalist narrative can contain features such as regional incubators, cluster formations, and joint work with development strategies to streamline the regional actors for the sake of making the region globally competitive (Cooke, 1992; Cooke et al., 2004).

Thus, while the grand narrative of new regionalism promotes a shift to competitiveness, autonomy, attractiveness, and innovation, it also fosters a policy strategy of cooperation within the regions (Keating, 2003). This de- velopment has had an impact on the role of regional authorities in the sense that they, to a greater extent, are thought of as facilitators for cooperation and strategic governance. This means that ideological differences should be put aside in order to be efficient in navigating the complex dynamics of intra-regional coordination. This new role is often referred to as a new 'regional leadership, where regional politics for development and growth is less a matter of conflict resolution and more a function to optimize the mechanisms of competitiveness and innovation. Stimson et al. (2002:279) describes it as:

> leadership for regional economic development will not be based on traditional hierarchical relationships; rather it will be a collaborative relationship between institutional actors encompassing the public, pri- vate and community sectors – and it will be based on mutual trust and co-operation.

In this new narrative, the role of politics and politicians does not primarily revolve around practices that can help channeling and acting out ideological conflicts by representing the voice or beliefs of their constituency. Rather, the new regionalism narrative promotes a leadership where strategizing, co- ordination, and cooperation for the 'good of everyone' are central features. In short, it is a role of transcending ideological conflict for the sake of competi- tiveness. In such circumstances, politics is viewed as problematic.

The need for knowledge and expertise

This book revolves around the meaning, function, and effect of knowledge and expertise in the context of regional development. It is clear that the conditions for regional development have undergone a quite dramatic trans- formation during the last decades, and we hold that the relationship between knowledge and expertise can be found at the center of this transformation in several ways.

First, this new global terrain of the flows of capital and resources seems to be an unpredictable place where knowledge and understanding about its

mechanisms and the ability to predict trends are an incredibly valuable resource for anyone looking to make successful strategic choices and priorities.
The need for knowledge about global economic dynamics and theories about
the mechanisms of economic growth has been closely intertwined with the
policy field of regional development. Scholarly work within economics, human geography, political science, and sociology is seen as important expertise in relation to policy development. From a governmentality perspective,
this mode of knowledge production and the role of expertise can be seen
as an expression of how the global terrain of regional development is being
rendered technical, or made governable – through producing meaning and
articulating rationalities that construe what is possible, sensible, and desirable.
In Chapter 3 we examine this aspect of knowledge and expertise through an
in-depth analysis of the significance of competition and competitiveness as a
master rationality for regional development.

Second, the new reasonability and mandate for regions to facilitate competiveness requires knowledge about how to navigate the complex dynamics
of internal global flows and preferences and internal dynamics of attractiveness. Regions find themselves in the complicated nexus of globalized
capitalism on one hand and local populations, institutions, and markets on
the other. The need for knowledge about how to merge these complex dynamics through working policy models seems urgent. The cost of falling
behind could be potentially devastating. This mode of knowledge production is closely related to the concept of governmental technologies – the
instruments, mechanisms, and apparatuses – used to navigate within the
field of governing and at the same time articulating the political rationalities
of the grand narrative of regional development. In Chapter 4 we examine
such governmental technologies; more precisely we study the importance of
numerical devices and their role in governing activities such as learning and
benchmarking.

Third, the internal dynamics, as they are articulated in the narrative of
new regionalism, call for policy knowledge that transcends the ideological
bias of political parties. Such knowledge is desired to be neutral, unbiased, free from ideological smokescreens, or petty self-interests. In this
sense, the need for external, unbiased expertise seems crucial for successful
policy development. In Chapter 5 we approach this mode of knowledge
with questions about how subjectivities are produced in relation to such
policies for regional development. How are the roles of social actors articulated from a perceived un-biased position embedded in the grand narrative described in this chapter? We pay attention to who is included and
excluded, and how social actors are made meaningful through the lens of
global competitiveness.

We present this grand narrative to give a first broad image of the basic
notions and assumptions that structure the policy- and scholarly field of regional development. In the following chapters, we will go deeper into these
dynamics as we move our empirical analysis forward.

Note

1 When we refer to the empirical material that have been analyzed and are used in this book for illustrations we have assigned each quote with a number that corresponds with the document in the table in Appendix 1. Many of the quotes have been translated into English by us.

3 Rationalities

We are at one of these conferences again. By now we have been attending several of them. Sometimes as experts – researchers invited to share our knowledge and to point out directions. Other times as observers, like now. You see, over the past decade our research team has grown increasingly interested in events such as this one. A large, annual gathering for analysts, strategists, consultants, researchers, and people who work with regional development. Gradually we have come to understand these conferences, award ceremonies, and deliberative gatherings as very important for the governing of this policy field. In the keynotes and the workshops, during the lunches, coffee breaks and dinners as well as in the hotel lobbies, the bars, and the taxis, political rationalities become visible. Not only visible. They take shape here. Form through the interactions between the bodies, subjects, and material entities that carry them. Steer, guide, and mark trajectories that reach far beyond this local context. So, therefore, we are here. To study this. At the same time we are a part of it. This is hard. One of us is hosting a workshop later on in the afternoon and we struggle with reflexivity, ethics, and methodology. Yet, we are convinced that there is something to be made of this immersion. This participation. So we move on. Take our seats. And the first plenary session starts.

One after another they enter and leave the stage. They speak. About competition and competitiveness. We listen. Take notes. Record with eyes and ears. After the keynote speakers are done its time for questions and comments. Instructions are given. There is a microphone clad in foam rubber, deliberately made into a form of 'speaker box.' People in the audience are instructed to toss it around to each other and raise questions. There are laughs and remarks about the microphone. It lightens up the discussion. Yet, the topic is serious. Some would even say grim. It concerns competition. A competition that is fierce and seems to always be there. It is local, regional, national, and global. The analysts and strategists in the audience reinforce it through their questions. However, someone is critical. She asks questions about winners and losers. Can we afford to have parts of the country as losers? How can we even speak like this? Can a part of the country just close down? Isn't that an unavoidable consequence of competition? People nod. Confirming whispers begin to form. But the microphone has been tossed. Another question takes form and the critique takes a shape that people are more comfortable with. The strategist with the microphone now instead asks us to think about how losing regions can make themselves into winners. And the discussion continues with suggestions. Best practice alternatives. Learning. Yet, under competition.

One of us notices something in the discussion among the analysts. She has been thinking about this before. Later she formulates it explicitly to the rest of us: "They are speaking as if they are at war. This competition. It sounds like a state of war. Listen to the words they use. I don't think they are aware of it themselves, yet they use them. All the time. Those militaristic references. This is important. And it is no side effect. To me it sounds like one of the most vital parts of this governing. To avoid annihilation." We agree. And so, we study it.

Develop or die

Mobilize your forces! Form alliances! Develop spearhead technology! Act strategically! Organize a united front! The militarized rhetoric within the discourse of regional competitiveness is striking as it formulates the conditions for the 'survival' of places, cities, and regions throughout Europe in an era of globalization. Here, 'the global' emerges as a threatening terrain where the capacity to attract resources in terms of creative, entrepreneurial people and capricious mobile capital are the best available fortifications in the inevitable battles for prosperity and growth to come (Mitander, 2015; Öjehag Pettersson, 2015; Peck, 2005; Säll, 2014). Through very specific representations of globalization, where global competition is articulated as a force of nature, the discourse positions its trajectories beyond the reach of politics, and therefore, to participate in the battle for resources is not a choice to make – it is inescapable. Like in traditional wars, this discourse also centers on the function of territory as vitally important. However, rather than defending national borders, the nature of the battles here requires that territory must be reimagined and restructured into a mosaic of competing sub-national entities to allow for a complex system of flows, where threats can be kept out while reinforcements simultaneously can enter. In the social sciences, this ongoing transformation has been recognized both in terms of a 'competition state' (eg. Brenner, 2004; Cerny, 1997; Jessop, 2002) as well as under the umbrella category 'resurgent regions' (cf. Cox, 2009; Keating, 2003; Lobao et al., 2009) that we described in the previous chapter.

Regardless of theoretical context, however, throughout the different research projects we have been involved with over the past decade, this notion of competitiveness really stands out. Indeed, we would identify it as the main political rationality governing regional development today. This may or may not be surprising, depending on the reader's background and experience, but suffice to say that it permeates everything from work related to gender equality (Öjehag-Pettersson, 2017) to issues of citizenship (Mitander, 2015) as well as learning, measuring, and benchmarking (Öjehag-Pettersson, 2019). Thus, in this chapter we aim to illustrate this master rationality of competitiveness as it manifests in regional development today. That being said, we actually find it even more important to consider the effects in terms of rationalities it gives rise to in turn. In particular, we argue that these rationalities are effects of and for expertise. Indeed, they lay out a grid of relations that not only are articulated by experts and through expert publications but also demand particular forms of expertise in the quest for competitiveness.

Staying with the militaristic and acute sense of urgency often communicated in the discourse, as illustrated in the vignette and beginning of this chapter, we describe three main political rationalities that, we argue, are effects of the master rationality of competitiveness. As mentioned, in our experience, and through the data we have generated in various circumstances, the quest to be competitive carries over into a wide range of practices and settings connected to regional development. As it turns out, we find that the militaristic rhetoric of the master rationality also lends itself well to describing the main effects. Thus, first, we stress that a main rationality that emerges in response to intense global competition in regional development is *the rationality of strategos*. This, we argue, is a salient rationality that concerns leadership and how regions should be governed more generally. Thus, it sets out particular directions for what it means to act strategically in the quest for competitiveness and also who best embodies the qualities needed for this. In other words, the rationality also designates a particular form of leadership as it nominates stakeholders and interests of importance in regional development. Thus, it names the strategos, the high ranking officers in the struggle.

We label the second rationality that we reconstruct from our data and current research as *the rationality of triage*. We use it to capture and designate how in the governing of regional development, there is a persistent tension also in the sense that it follows logically from a situation where competition reigns supreme, that there will be winners and losers. This presents policy makers and other expressions of expertise with a particular problem. What is to be made of the losers? And what about the winners? In this sense, we argue that the prevailing rationality in contemporary regional development resembles that of the classic medical procedure of triage, where surgeons and medical professionals working with scarce conditions under acute circumstances (such as war) make decisions in line with certain ethical and logical convictions.

Third, and finally, we trace what we identify as *the rationality of intelligence*. This captures the plethora of features in regional development pertaining to benchmarking, measuring, gauging, and learning. In short, this is one of the most prominent expressions of expertise where scientific methods and techniques are highlighted as important tools in the broader machinery that can be set into motion to achieve competitiveness.

In sum then, this chapter will focus on what we consider a master rationality in regional development, namely competition and competitiveness. In addition, we draw out how this produces other rationalities as responses to the question 'how do we best become competitive.' In the next section, we introduce how the rationality of competition and competitiveness is articulated throughout contemporary regional development; however, before we turn to empirical illustrations, we take the time to consider how the development of this rationality has been described by researchers.

Competition and competitiveness as governmental problems

Notions of competition between territories have been cataloged in the academic literature since at least the 1950s when economist Tiebout (1956) argued that certain amounts of competition among local governments would contribute to more efficient spending of public funds. However, while Tiebout had formulated a theory that suggested to increase competition, the adoption of such ideas among policy makers was slow. Indeed, it was not until the late 1980s that researchers such as David Harvey (1989) started to describe how states and sub-national territories alike increasingly were being governed through 'entrepreneurial' policies. From the beginning, these policies were articulated as part of specific understandings of the emerging phenomenon of globalization (Ohmae, 1993, 1996), and this intertwined relation between globalization studies and urban and regional studies continues even today (Öjehag-Pettersson, 2015). Even more generally, the advancement of ideas and policies that advocate territorial competition can also be understood as part and parcel of the widespread promotion of market-oriented practices and neoliberal modes of governing that marked the last decades of political development throughout the world. In this sense, the Tiebout principle could be made operational only after neoliberal modes of governing were made more universally acceptable. In this circumstance, it is also important to notice how the rise of policies that promote territorial competition, since the days of Tiebout, has been characterized by blurred boundaries between policy making and scholarly work, producing situations that one scholar has called 'theory led by policy' (Lovering, 1999).

The kind of entrepreneurial policies noticed and described by Harvey (1989) in the late 1980s paved the way for what other scholars coined 'the competition state' (Cerny, 1997, 1999; Dicken, 2011; Jessop, 2002, 2015; Rinehart, 1995). They did so after turning their attention to how the globalizing processes at the time, such as a transnational and 'footloose' finance capital as well as growing transnational regimes, seemed to trigger a response among states who struggled to reformulate their possibilities to intervene in the economic and social reality of their respective political systems. In the course of this progression the long hailed idea of competition among firms and corporations was transposed onto states, cities, and regions which produced a new edifice where capitalist logic and development could merge fully with state policy. Thus, according to Cerny (1997), the focus among states and regions shifted from an ambition to secure employment, redistribute income, and provide social services to instead strive for policies that would foster innovation and entrepreneurship. To be sure, as noted by many scholars (cf. Fougner, 2006; Jessop, 2002) this was not a development that unfolded in exactly the same ways all over the world. Instead, different articulations of territorial competition and the competitiveness of states and regions emerged where, for instance, traditionally social democratic states would differ from liberal states, which, in turn, differed from the strong state technocracy – sometimes denoted *dirigisme*. However, this does not change the fact that for all of them the notion of competitiveness as a virtue for states, regions, and cities was installed as more or less a necessity and it was 'hammered home by governments, corporations, and the media to the point that it is taken for granted, a fact of life that is so obvious that we unthinkingly acquiesce to its dictates' (Rinehart, 1995:14).

Given that territorial competition and 'the competition state' are such prolific concepts within the academic literature and in policy circles, it is also relevant to consider the notion of competitiveness somewhat further. So far, it has been used here without much qualification, but if territorial competition denotes a condition in which states, regions, and cities must behave like firms and corporations to secure prosperity, then competitiveness denotes the means through which they may succeed. Thus, there is clearly a close relationship not only conceptually between a world marked by competition among territorial units and the same units' quests for competitiveness. Rather, ideas of how to achieve competitiveness have, in practice, been entangled with the very notion of territorial competition from the onset. Indeed, policies directed towards competitiveness and their accompanied technologies of measurement and benchmarking seem vital to sustain the idea of competition in the first place (Bruno, 2009).

As states scrambled to become competitive they turned to the business schools, and in this way some of the most influential works so far in contemporary regional governance were published (Bristow, 2005). Michael E. Porter's The Competitive Advantage of Nations (1990) is the prime example, and the concept of 'clusters' would go on to become something of a global policy discourse on its own (cf. Säll, 2012, 2014). The importation of business models and the increased focus on fostering competitive environments at different spatial scales (Jessop, 2002; Peck, 2002; Peck & Tickel, 2002) can be said to be one aspect of the still ongoing territorial transformations of state space, and while there are a range of others, the search for a 'new institutional fix' (Peck & Tickel, 1994) that best enables the production of competitiveness is probably one of the most important.

The combination of this search for a new institutional fix and the business school models for competitiveness became intertwined with ongoing policy formulations, not least various initiatives of the European Union. Together they aligned in their promotion of sub-national regions as the most suitable territorial formation for fostering competitive environments in an era of global competition (cf. Keating, 1998). It was in the regions, and particularly in the metropolitan city regions, that the key to success in the looming battles for resources were to be found. Consequently, in the words of Storper (1997:3) the scholarly conception of the region shifted from being understood as 'an outcome of deeper political-economic processes' to something that 'might be a fundamental basis of economic and social life'.

To sum up, competition and competitiveness emerge as governmental problems for states in relation to what is often identified as globalization as well as in the wake of neoliberal modes of governing. Following Bacchi (2009) and more general governmentality studies we argue that we find in policy, implicit and powerful representations of the problem at hand, which can be used as a point of departure for analyzing politics more broadly. Thus, as we turn to empirical illustrations, drawing from data generated over the last decade in different research projects, we aim to sketch the contours of how competition and competitiveness become intertwined with our notion of traveling expertise. Moreover, this allows us to draw out implications of these representations and enables us to set up for the remainder of the chapter where we analyze the main political rationalities that govern regional development today.

Competition and competitiveness in contemporary regional development

Notions of competition and competitiveness are articulated continuously throughout regional development today. It is, as mentioned, more or less always present, regardless of the issue that is being discussed. That being said, there are also patterns and themes in terms of *how* it is articulated. As a political rationality, it rests upon three implicit and intertwined assumptions:

1   That global competition is a natural and unavoidable expression of a more global world.
2   That economic growth is the foundation for human development.
3   That competitiveness is key to achieve better relative growth than others, which, in the end, matters more than absolute growth.

Together, these underlying assumptions steer the content of the discussions in regional development, and therefore they are important to consider before moving on to some of the effects associated with the competitiveness rationality.

Beginning with the first point, we regard this as very important. Globalization is often pointed to in regional development as the key driver behind a development where sub-national regions are now becoming global actors to a much greater extent than before. When doing so, they also reproduce what in scholarly work often is identified as a *globalist* view of what globalization is and how it functions (Öjehag-Pettersson, 2015). In short, this position emphasizes how globalization is the first step in a new world order, where the importance of nations will wither away and where regions, particularly metropolitan city regions, will take the leading place in driving human development. Moreover, in this take, globalization is an inevitable consequence of technological development and liberalization of the world economy in terms of increased trade and economic exchange. Financial capital and information are understood to flow freely across an increasingly borderless space and large firms, the so called Multi-National Corporations (MNCs), become pivotal players, changing the game for politics. Obviously, there are variations to these expressions, and no regions that we have studied operate under the assumption that the nation state is going to be unimportant in the foreseeable future. That being said, when regions try to articulate the foundation for why they find themselves competing, they often do so in terms of this rather simplified understanding of globalization.

Interestingly, in this search for a foundation for competition and competitiveness, regions help reconfigure the ontological position of globalization as a process. It moves from the realm of politics and decision making into what we may call a natural realm. It becomes less a matter of human activity that can be changed through politics and much more of a natural phenomenon to which we *have to* relate. In this sense, globalization, and by extension its prime effect – global competition – resembles a tsunami or an earthquake. Like with such phenomena of nature, politics need to be prepared to handle globalization, however, to try and change it at its core seems foolish and un-informed. It is simply the way things work. In conjunction with the way that globalization is equated with trade, finance, and technology, this helps position territorial competition as a natural state of things and thus, competition and competitiveness become hegemonic concepts, forming a master rationality. Consider the quote below from what used to be the Swedish national strategy for regional growth from the year 2014:

> Globalization is a process which makes national borders less significant as communication, trade and access to other countries increase and job markets and economies become more and more integrated. This process entails both opportunities and challenges for regions, businesses and individuals. The workforce is increasingly mobile, not least in the Nordic region and between the EU countries where the job market is free. As a result, there is an influx of foreign labor to the Swedish job market, at the same time as many Swedish people choose to work abroad. Global financial competition increases the pressure to reorganize the economy. At the same time, there is an increase not only in capital flow and investments, but also in trade, travel, and migration. Moreover, we see an intensified exchange of information and technology.
>
> (02:6)

This description is indicative of contemporary regional development as arguments for competitiveness are constructed. In more detailed reports and publications by experts such as consultants and academics, this more general and broad description of globalization is often explicitly linked to territorial competition. One important actor in this regard is the European Spatial Planning Observation Network (ESPON) which is an applied research program funded by the EU (or rather the EC) with the goal to produce systematic and reliable territorial evidence with policy makers as the main target group. Broadly, they aim to contribute to the EU cohesion policy. A salient theme in their reports and publications is the increased competitiveness for EU regions to survive in a competitive world. The quote below from one of their reports published in 2013 shows this explicit link:

> Transnational firms operate in more than one country at a time and are considered as some of the most powerful economic and political entities in the globalized world economy. The economic success of cities in conditions of growing competition depends on their capability to attract and retain investment capital of transnational corporations, which allow urban areas to be included in the network of global connections. That explains why there is a strong competition between individual cities, manifested in creating remarkable conditions in order to attract the headquarters of transnational companies in each one of them.
>
> (03:21)

As mentioned, one of the most common tropes in this narrative of competitiveness is, like in the quote above from ESPON, about being attractive for various forms of flows and mobile resources. In particular, to be attractive for international investment capital and expert citizens is both a means and an end in the quest for competitiveness. It is a proof that you are doing something right and that you are at the same time positioning yourself even better for the continued efforts in the harsh competition. The Nordic Council of Ministers (NCM) sums this view up like this:

> In the global economy, no economy can compete based on its own inherent resources and capabilities alone. It also needs to attract investment capital, human capital, and ideas. And it has to retain its own companies and people as far as they can choose where to invest or live and work. Attracting global interest is both an indicator and enabler of global competitiveness, just like the ability to see internationally: Only competitive locations are able to attract foreign interest. And the inflow of foreign capital and skills makes a location more competitive.
>
> (04:37)

Taken together the three quotes above illustrate how discourses of globalization are a prominent part in the formation of contemporary political rationalities for governing regional development. While this may be so, the take away point here is the way that this process is naturalized. Notice how in all of the quotes globalization quickly becomes a matter of global competition. Moreover, as it is articulated this seems to be a phenomena that just happens. It is very seldom connected to particular actors or forms of action that can be made the object of political programs. Instead, legitimization for a strive towards competitiveness is anchored in rational, scientific explanations of what seem to be a natural phenomenon rather than a product of certain political choices. Indeed, this is a rather common way to seek discursive legitimization for any argument today (Van Leeuwen, 2007). However, in this case it is also interesting to note how such rationalistic and scientific articulations are mixed with narratives that work through other forms of legitimization. In particular, the documents, interviews, observations, and media articles that are part of our extensive data are filled with narratives that resemble classic tales or stories in the sense that they contain heroes, villains, threats, moments of glory, and a sense of overcoming great obstacles. These *mythic* articulations also serve as legitimization, and we argue that they become particularly powerful when combined with the scientific and rationalistic ways of legitimizing the central position of competition in regional development.

In short, the general and implicit assumptions connected to the competitiveness rationality can be described as follows. Since globalization primarily is a process that brings with it intense competition, not only between firms but also between territorial units such as nations, regions, and cities, to be competitive is not a choice. It is a natural response to a natural threat. For any region that wish to fulfill its function of producing growth, which in turn is the foundation for being able to sustain a good life in the region, to be competitive is simply vital. It doesn't seem to be enough with just growth. Any given region must be concerned with if it is growing faster than others and if it is more competitive than others. This gives rise to additional rationalities directed towards *how to be competitive*. Indeed, as described in the beginning of this chapter, while we consider the rationality of competitiveness to be a form of master rationality for the entire paradigm of regional development, we find it very important to describe the effects it has. Among these effects, we argue, are three main political rationalities that all are intertwined with competition and competitiveness in precisely the sense that they help set out directions and plot trajectories for how to be the best region. Taken together, they give rise to and enable various forms of traveling expertise, and indeed, they are also sustained by this expertise as it takes physical form as consultants, academics or the particularly desired creative and entrepreneurial subjects that are understood as very important in regional development. In the following, we stick with the militaristic discourse that we drew on initially in this chapter as we flesh out the rationality of triage, the rationality of strategos, and the rationality of intelligence.

The rationality of strategos

One of the primary and the most salient political rationalities that are formed in relation to competition and competitiveness concerns leadership. Here, we designate it *the rationality of strategos* alluding to the old Greek word for high ranking military officers. Indeed, just as in warfare or business, contemporary regional development is quite centered on the strategic opportunities made possible by the leadership, the strategos. In this sense, this is a rationality that deals with two aspects. On the one hand, much effort is directed towards the composition of the leadership as such. This means that this political rationality articulates specific notions of *what* regional leadership actually should be, *how* it should work as well as *who* should be included. On the other hand, this rationality also designates the strategic operations that would help optimize the leadership as well as points out a set of interventions, priorities, and policy agendas that are vital for success in the global competition.

Leadership: what, how, who?

The question of how regional competitiveness should be governed is closely related to how the regional leadership should be organized – who should be included among the strategos? A prominent feature in this regard is how regional leadership derives political authority in the various forms of data that we have generated throughout our different projects. Their primary legitimacy comes from being selected, or maybe recruited, to use a term that is sometimes applied in policy formulations, as the protectors of prosperity in the regions. For instance, the strategos are usually represented in terms of 'stake-holders' or 'the affected,' leaders from 'business/industries,' 'the public sector,' and 'universities,' and in some contexts 'the civil society' and 'interest groups' of any given region. In other words, we are not dealing with a typical political leadership in the sense of elected representatives that are accountable to the public in the traditional way of representative democracy. Rather, to put it blunt, the strategos are the important people and entities of the region and they have a legitimate claim to leadership precisely because they are important. Indeed, to deploy a more traditional (political) leadership is often seen as problematic, because politics tend to be ineffective from this point of view. Instead, the leadership should pull in the same direction, not squabble over ideological differences or petty disagreements. The goal here is to come together and lead the region towards competitiveness. Consider, for instance, how this is formulated in the so called Regional Development Strategy (RDS) of a Swedish region:

> Regional development and growth efforts are so complex that nobody can manage on their own. It is necessary to cooperate and collaborate, both across political domains and between the regional and local levels. Many agents in different roles take part. Leadership on different levels is required in order to create and develop alliances between key partners in order to implement the Dalarna strategy. Regional development is in a sense the sum total of local developments. In other words, regional development cannot happen unless the local level is involved. Municipal and local leadership capabilities are therefore especially crucial for the objectives of the Dalarna strategy to be realized. Leadership is a prerequisite and a key factor for success when it comes to the potential results of regional strategies. Consequently, it is important that the regional

leadership can run development efforts in such a way that the necessary focus on a few strategically important challenges is maintained. Tactical games in which different agents block each other or try to displace the responsibility for what happens onto others should be avoided.

(05:25)

Again, this rationality carries an implicit and explicit critique towards party politics as part of regional development. Instead, the regional leadership is usually described using prefixes such as 'decisive,' 'strong,', 'unified,' and 'united,' In broad terms, the strategos are to act like the generals they are and strive to 'mobilize a mutual frontier' towards external 'threats.' Here, like in war time, politics is problematic. Instead, in order to be competitive there should be others who help to oversee the struggle. The OECD, for instance, points out how the regional leadership should make room for those who actually contribute most to competitiveness and growth – private actors. Sticking with the Swedish example for a moment, consider how the OECD encourages Sweden to include private actors in the formulation of its regional development strategies:

> While private actors are clearly involved in the financing of regional policy, their role in designing regional strategies appears more limited, although progress has been made with the implementation of the regional growth policy. Former NUTEK, now Tillväxtverket [The Swedish Agency for Economic and Regional Growth] has played a role in stimulating co-operation with private actors in the design of regional development and growth programs (RUPs and RTPs), which encourage counties to establish regional partnerships that include private stakeholders. However, the participation of private companies in the design of programs remains limited (Tillväxtverket, 2008). This is partly due to lack of time and resources and the fact that they do not see the benefits for themselves of participating. Regional leaders have a critical role in ensuring enhanced public-private co-operation on the design of a regional strategy/vision for regional growth (current RUPs), based on regional comparative advantages.

(06:231)

Over the last couple of decades, a range of policy models have been deployed that, to a varying degree, capture this idea of a regional leadership comprised of stakeholders and interest groups rather than elected officials. For instance, regional partnerships, innovation systems, and triple (or quadruple) helix models as well as clusters are some examples that have been influential throughout Europe and beyond. While the models and concepts differ, they have in common precisely the idea that a region needs to gather its most important businesses, policy makers, agencies, and institutions and have them focus on a number of prioritized goals. This brings us to the second aspect of this rationality.

Strategic alliances

As the regional leadership form around the strategos, it is clear that it must be able to broker strategic alliances and complex cooperation. By complex we mean that cooperation is conditioned upon the threat of competition and it should be conducted in such ways that it maximizes the regions' own competitiveness. This means that cooperation could be about different agents within the region aligning their interests and coordinating their efforts through, for instance, clusters, but it could also be a matter of cross regional alliances. Such alliances could form within a country, but through, for instance, various EU initiatives the rationality of strategos also promotes international cooperation. This is often particularly important in so called border regions where the leadership often is thought to be able to boost the competitiveness and development of their region if they can find strategic partners on the other side of the border. Another example from a Swedish region and their regional development strategy is indicative, not only for the Swedish or the Nordic case but also for Europe and beyond:

> A cross-border regional leadership capable of mobilizing agents, prioritizing, and implementing long-term efforts is crucially important for the future development of the region. Regional agents like political organizations, the business sector, universities, the county administrative board and interest groups must work together and cooperate to realize a common agenda. The region needs to claim a space on both national and international arenas, and a united front will facilitate that effort. Cooperation on local, national and European levels is simplified if there is a clear regional leadership capable of handling uncertainty about the future and balancing the many agents that together promote regional development. In a world which changes quickly and where we do not know what is going to happen or what will be required in the future, we need a strong leadership that can harness and augment the regional potential of the county.
>
> (07:9)

This complexity means that something that in one circumstance is articulated as a particularly challenging threat could be transformed into a strategic opportunity in another circumstance. Thus, the leadership need to broker these alliances continuously and also be ready to import knowledge and skills from the allies. Some examples, like China, are particularly ambiguous. It should come as no surprise that China is an important actor in the global competitive environment. Its impact on regional development is felt throughout Europe and it is commonly viewed as both a threat and an opportunity. With the right strategos in place, dealing with China could be very beneficial. Consider again a formulation from the Nordic Council of Ministers:

> China has witnessed a dramatic increase in its research and innovative capacities in the past decade, with far-reaching implications for the global

knowledge and innovation geography. The Nordic countries are principally well positioned both to compete and cooperate with China, particularly in the field of climate and energy. However clearer strategies and better models for cooperation are required, particularly at national and university level, to allow the Nordic countries to realize this potential.

(04:7)

In sum then, the rationality of strategos is connected to the master rationality of competitiveness by explicitly formulating the need for a particular leadership. This leadership should be able to hammer out differences that may exist within the region and get disparate actors to pull in the same direction. It should also be able to create temporary alliances and cooperation formats that are beneficial for the region in the long run. In other words, the leadership really does resemble that of an army in wartime or, perhaps a bit less drastic, the management of a private firm competing on a market. Clearly, it is not a leadership based in politics. We will get back to a discussion of this later, however, for now suffice to say that a wealth of research has shown that regions under such conditions become spaces of depoliticization, where relations of power are concealed (Rönnblom, 2008), informal networks spur (Forsberg & Lindgren, 2010), and consensus becomes a prerequisite for politics rather than an effect of it (Säll, 2012:107). Next, we turn to one of the most fundamental tasks that the strategos deal with, namely, what kind of sacrifices are needed in the quest for competitiveness?

The rationality of triage

We argue that a second salient effect of governing for competitiveness in regional development is *the rationality of triage*. By using this label, we mean to highlight how even though notions of extreme competition are so central, there is a strong tendency to gloss over the fact that sacrifices must be made and that competition usually means that we will end up with winners and losers. We argue that while this may be glossed over and while most policies simultaneously seem to portray the idea that competition is extremely harsh and that the future is bright for all regions, there is an implicit rationality that emerges in texts as well as practice. This rationality articulates how the competition and the subsequent measures taken to produce competitiveness actually will require sacrifices as well as a redirection of resources to fortify the most important strongholds. Again, we capture this thinking using the concept of triage.

Triage has been an important medical practice to make sensible priorities with scarce resources in war and under other disastrous conditions. By assigning the wounded soldiers in categories as either (1) likely to live regardless of treatment, (2) likely to live if treated, and (3) likely to die even if treated, the field surgeons could find a specific ethical rationale for making priorities under catastrophic circumstances and strict scarcity. Triage as rationality related to regional development and its quest for competitiveness raise questions of how dimensions of prioritization and selection are manifested as aspects of the state of insecurity regions understand themselves to be in. While they are not actually on a battlefield dealing with wounded soldiers, triage, with some adjustments, describe quite well how prioritization is made. We argue that this rationality articulates such priorities along three different axes. First, triage is applied in relation to political objectives that could be viable for a region to pursue. Second, it is applied with respect to how places should be prioritized and, third, to what groups of people that are important and less important for competitiveness.

Triage with respect to political objectives

First then, in terms of political objectives, we have already been addressing this aspect somewhat when discussing the master rationality of competitiveness above. Recall how competitiveness is understood to be a foundation for producing growth, which, in turn, is a prerequisite for developing society at all. In relation to political objectives and ambitions the rationality of triage highlights this aspect. Thus, it is often so that the rationality of competitiveness intertwines with the rationality of triage and the rationality of strategos to legitimize how certain political objectives, even if desirable, are not feasible, while others are. The cut throat environment of global competition construes the regional leadership as one that must make hard priorities in order to optimize the capacity of attracting resources. Even though other political objectives are viewed as important, they are reinterpreted in a hierarchal relation to the strive for competitiveness. Some are simply seen as beyond rescue, while others are devoted attention and resources to make them work under conditions of global competition.

In several different national contexts, one policy area that is often brought up for discussion and reinvention is health care. Now, a caveat is needed here since there are some important differences in health care systems throughout Europe; however, generally speaking, in regional development health care is often understood as a challenge and an untapped potential. Again, in general, this means that if given sufficient treatment it can be reinvented as something that can boost innovation and entrepreneurship, two important means towards competitiveness. Thus, universal, publicly funded health care is important for the people of a city, a region or a country, however, under conditions of harsh competition it needs to be reimagined in important ways. If this shows how competitiveness functions as a precondition for health care another important way to understand this relationship is the view that health is one of the most important factors for the private sector to maintain a competent workforce. In other words, health care, like many other policy areas, is assessed not only on its own merits and importance, but also in terms of how well it can contribute to the production of competitiveness and growth. In this sense the rationality of triage in regional leadership becomes a way to categorize and prioritize political objectives as they become meaningful in the regional state of insecurity.

Triage with respect to places and spaces

Another important aspect of the rationality of triage regards the prioritization of places within regions. Striving for global attractiveness calls for a concentration of resources to urban centers that are understood as regional 'growth engines' and 'nodes' for development. Urban areas are particularly important keys as they can generate critical masses of talent, capital, creativity, innovation, entrepreneurship, and infrastructure to be globally competitive. This urban prerogative entails a specific understanding of the value of different parts of a region. The quote below illustrates how this rationality is manifested in a report on regional competitiveness commissioned by a public agency and carried out by a large international consultancy firm:

> Benefits for competitiveness from a new geography can only arise if there is a capacity to view the development of the region in a holistic way and let the parts of the region with the best conditions for competitiveness take the full advantage of those conditions. Other parts of the region have to successively increase their integration with the region's growth center and its vicinity.
>
> (08:9)

Thus, through the rationality of competitiveness intertwined with the rationality of triage a rendering of hierarchically situated places and spaces within regions is made possible. To be sure, most countries have been structured around a center-periphery relation for a long time. However, while earlier much of regional policy actually was devoted to programs designed to level out differences, the current situation actively promotes a reinforcement of the prosperous and competitive places. In practice, this means that large metropolitan areas are the ones that benefit most from the current policies. Therefore, what is actually a quite explicit power relation and political situation, that between urban and rural parts of regions, becomes depoliticized as part of the necessary and 'natural' triage needed to prosper in the global competition. More generally, all places are constantly under this triage logic as in the final analysis, their importance is measured by their relative contribution to competitive regional mobilization and unification under unsecure global conditions. Moreover, the scale is important here in the sense that what in one context is a given, dominant urban center, is in another circumstance a peripheral city in need of special attention if, at all, it shall have a chance to survive. In effect, this means that there are very few places that can be classified as such that they will survive even if not treated (as in classic triage). Rather, here triage is recast so that the already prosperous and successful places are still seen as in need of treatment. In short, prioritizing the center on behalf of the periphery is articulated as a necessary part of the greater good and at the same time also the best possible option for the periphery to survive in the long run, like leaving the wounded behind in order to win the war.

Triage with respect to people

A third way in which the rationality of triage manifests itself in the regional leadership is in the selective articulations of people. In the same ways that political objectives and places are prioritized through assessment of their capacity to contribute to competitiveness, so are the regional populations. Specific characteristics such as high education, mobility, creativity, and entrepreneurship are understood as directly linked to competitiveness. This is the part of the regional population that must be prioritized. As articulated in the same report by the global consultancy firm as above:

> The creative people of the future will be attracted to the most stimulating and tolerant environments they can find. They will be much more mobile than today and the competition for them will increase. Attractiveness has come in as a regional factor for competition directed towards people, businesses and capital. The capacity to attract 'the best' and thereby get ahead in an all the more specialized global competition is increasingly emphasized.
>
> (08)

The parts of the population that is unable to contribute to any of the competitive characteristics are instead articulated not only as undeserving, but also as actual threats that must be handled. In the quote below, from a county report, the part of the population with low education is discussed:

> Even more serious for the economic development and the corporations' ability to maintain competitiveness is the low level of education [...] This in combination with lacking communications poses as threats to the corporation's possibility to attract competence and capital. [...] In order to counteract this development steps have to be taken to attract highly educated people from other places in Sweden and the world.
>
> (09)

Thus, in sum, like when the disastrous conditions of the battlefield drove the field surgeons to develop an ethics of selection and prioritization, the rationality of triage in regional development helps the leadership to select, categorize, and prioritize political objectives, places, and people through the specific ethics that emerge in the global competition.

The rationality of intelligence

In this final political rationality that we present in this chapter we turn our attention to the intelligence gathering, which is considered vital for success in the global competition. More specifically, this rationality of intelligence articulates the need for expertise very clearly and directly points towards certain practices such as benchmarking, measurement, evaluation, and comparison as important. While this theme is one expression of this rationality, we also argue that it has a facet that is more directed towards the actual composition of the kind of regions that can be made prosperous in future struggles. In short, so called SMART specialization and SMART cities and regions are reoccurring themes that have been made increasingly salient in regional development during the most recent years, and here we aim to address it as part of the rationality of intelligence.

Benchmarking, evaluation, and comparison

Forestalling the discussion of the next chapter somewhat, there is a very pronounced notion of policy as evaluable in contemporary regional development. This means that policy makers are encouraged to design programs with clearly stated goals that are possible to measure and evaluate over a specific time period. As part of this, expertise in the form of *external experts* become very important as they are seen not only as legitimate evaluators that can provide 'sound' assessments but also as vehicles for evidence based policy making. In other words, this kind of expertise lends itself to legitimizing processes for the practices conducted by policymakers, and at the same time they can help with designing everything from workshops and seminars to comprehensive programs of policy learning. One straight forward example of how this expertise is promoted in regional development is provided by the EU in the context of discussing cohesion and territorial policy:

> Involving territorial experts when a sector policy is being formulated could enhance territorial cohesion by the integration of territorial information into sector activities. An even deeper involvement is recommended in the case of regional and territorial policies. It is important to use the EU network of territorial experts, and to keep the European Commission informed about the availability of territorial experts. ESPON can already be a good starting point for setting up a European expert database and knowledge network and for making recommendations on territorial competences for educational and similar institutions.
>
> (11:88)

So, as the external expertise lend a form of legitimization to certain practices in regional development, they are often also enlisted to help with learning and augmentation of skills among policymakers in a given region. In this way, the external experts and policy makers are tied together. The primary tool used in this regard seems to be *benchmarking*. Recall the vignette of this chapter that describes a conference where the leading expertise and policymakers that are a part of this practice can meet and exchange ideas. This is a typical setting that is part and parcel of the maintenance and promotion of important political rationalities, which also allows them to be enacted, embodied, and performed. As we have already argued, such instances are important for benchmarking in broad terms; however, it is also important to recognize that the concept of benchmarking is articulated in such ways within regional development that it is clearly a multisided endeavor. Indeed, a range of concepts and practices such as auditing, standardizing, ranking, and learning can be grouped under the concept of benchmarking, which goes to show some of the variegated expressions this can have.

Taken together, however, the basic feature of benchmarking in regional development is to compare and contrast with the explicit goal of learning or improving whatever a given region is interested in. This practice originated in the automobile industry of Japan in the 1960s and soon after started to merge with similar thinking in American businesses under the label Total Quality Management (TQM). Interestingly, well into the 1980s benchmarking within this context was directed inwards and had no outward looking ambition. In other words, it was a way for corporations to rather narrowly secure and control the quality of their production in its various steps and sequences, not to compare and rank themselves against competitors. However, as the discourse changed this became a much more pronounced feature, not least when it became part of the public sector under New Public Management. So, for regions, like most nation states, the concept of benchmarking may be articulated as one that helps learning, however, in practice it is much more about ranking and ordering for the purpose of gauging competitiveness (for a more in-depth discussion on the genealogy of Benchmarking see Larner & Le Heron, 2002).

We argue that this comparative feature of benchmarking is particularly important in relation to the rationality of intelligence since it actively sustains the master rationality of competitiveness. Put short, in order for competitiveness to manifest in the real it must be underpinned by these outward looking and comparative practices of benchmarking. Unlike other forms of contrasting and comparison, benchmarking, through hierarchical rankings and orderings, facilitates a relentless and perpetual struggle for regions to reinvent, restructure, and mobilize towards a moving target. As we shall see in the next chapter, this lies inherent in the practices of ranking and ordering when we analyze them as governmental technologies of central concern for traveling expertise and regional development. For now, however, we wish to also point out the second feature of this political rationality of intelligence, namely the articulation of SMART specialization and SMART cities/regions.

SMART specialization and SMART cities/regions

This second aspect of the rationality of intelligence is more directed to particular structures within regions that ideally should be in place in order to achieve higher competitiveness. Nevertheless, in this regard the notion of intelligence is still important. First, there is currently a strong promotion of so-called SMART specialization among European regions. In short, this is a program run by the European Commission that articulates a specific way for regions to work towards competitiveness. Essentially, this means that by working towards a strategy that involves the pinpointing and selection of limited aspects of certain sectors of local business and production, the region can find a way to capitalize off of its absolute advantages. The EC hosts a web portal called the Smart Specialization Platform, where they describe the approach like this:

> Conceived within the reformed Cohesion policy of the European Commission, Smart Specialization is a place-based approach characterized by the identification of strategic areas for intervention based both on the analysis of the strengths and potential of the economy and on an Entrepreneurial Discovery Process (EDP) with wide stakeholder involvement. It is outward-looking and embraces a broad view of innovation including but certainly not limited to technology-driven approaches, supported by effective monitoring mechanisms.
>
> (12)

Currently, over 180 European regions have opted to connect through the platform, which means that they have steered their regional development work towards the task of producing a smart specialization strategy. As they have done so, the EC provides tools and structures through which the regions can enlist expertise and work through benchmarking in order to continuously develop their strategy. Again, as they do so, it is paramount for them to work selectively, or in our terms in accordance with the rationality of triage:

> To have a strategy means to make choices for investment. Member states and regions ought to support only a limited number of well-identified priorities for knowledge-based investments and/or clusters. Specialization means focusing on competitive strengths and realistic growth potentials supported by a critical mass of activity and entrepreneurial resources.
>
> (13)

As regions deploy their SMART specialization strategy, it is a prime example of benchmarking in the sense discussed above, namely where the strive for learning actually propels the competitiveness rationality. Monitoring and evaluation is key for success, and it is interesting to note how regions incorporate academic practices such as 'peer review' (like the OECD has been doing for some time) where the idea is that regions help evaluate each other and open up their strategies for critique.

> Finally, a good strategy must include a sound monitoring and evaluation system as well as a revision mechanism for updating the strategic choices.
>
> (13)

Thus, the evaluation and monitoring works intertwined with the complex patterns of cooperation discussed above under 'The rationality of the strategos.' In a way, therefore, SMART specialization is a good example that showcases the interlinked notion of all three political rationalities that we describe here and how they combine to promote the master rationality of competitiveness.

Before we turn to a summarizing discussion of the rationalities that we have presented in this chapter and their relationships with travelling expertise, it is also worth noting a peculiar mix-up regarding the concept of SMART. While in regional development it first and foremost signifies the practice of developing the strategy accounted for above, with the rise of big data, algorithms, and a rapidly advancing information technology it also holds another meaning. Indeed, all over the world, cities and regions are also striving to become SMART in the sense that they try to activate technology even more than before. Now, artificial intelligence, robotic systems, and computerized decision making and a constantly connected internet of things combine in many policy formulations as a source of competitiveness ready to harness in the years to come. Here, like often in connection to the rationality of intelligence, external experts in the form of private consultants are important as vessels for the promotion of said rationality. In this case, many of the largest consultancy firms are actively working with their visions of future regions and cities. Through the rationality of intelligence these visions are already becoming intertwined with regional development, most likely expanding its frontiers significantly in the years to come.

In closing: rationalities for and of expertise

In this chapter we have showed how a master rationality that we have called the rationality of competitiveness is at work in regional development. In particular, we have highlighted how it is linked to the production of three major and interlinked additional rationalities – the rationality of strategos, the rationality of triage, and the rationality of intelligence. Together they bestow the field of regional development with qualities that help facilitate the sustenance and formation of the assemblage we have called travelling expertise. In addition, the rationalities we have described map well onto the general description we have made concerning new regionalism and the narratives of regional development that can be found in most current research.

Thus, we argue that our illustrations show how these rationalities help give room for various expressions of expertise. First, it is certainly so that all of the rationalities help promote the overall idea that regional development is a field that is best handled without politics or at least by a leadership that is not embodied by politicians. Rather, in the fierce struggle for competitiveness and a prominent position in the race for resources and talent, expertise in this regard takes the form of leadership. This can be exercised by a range of actors and institutions that together constitute what is sometimes referred to as *regional stakeholders*. In other words, representatives from important firms and businesses together with prominent actors from public sector institutions such as universities, agencies, and municipalities are supposed to form a leadership that first and foremost can *broker deals* and make the region united in its strive for competitiveness.

This particular expression of an *expert leadership*, rather than a political one, is further underpinned by the rationalities at work in the assemblage in as much that it seeks (and finds) legitimation both in its abilities to hammer out differences and make the hard decisions needed as articulated by the rationality of triage, as well as in the recommendations and reviews offered by the rationality of intelligence. In a way then, the rationalities produce a form of expertise that is self-sustainable. It refers to itself as the source of its existence. Sometimes this is very explicit. The strategos call out for intelligence, often asking for research or evaluations of a particular strategy. The intelligence answers and underlines the leadership's legitimacy and its appropriate ways of action. Decisions are made, as suggested by the rationality of triage.

Thus, as we have argued several times by now, these rationalities are both *of* and *for* expertise. While we could point to a number of additional effects beyond the production of a form of leadership as important (we have given several examples in this chapter), for now we take this to be a good indication of how expertise is formed and informs. Later, in the final chapter of this book we will return to a theorization of what we think is the main point with regard to traveling expertise in regional development, namely its depoliticizing effects. Before we can properly lay out such a discussion, however, we need to explore the technologies of expertise as well as the subjects and social actors that it produces. We begin with an illustration of some of the governmental technologies associated with the rationalities discussed here.

4   Technologies

We have learned to use caveats in situations like these. So, this time was no different. Right after introducing ourselves and the title of our presentation we spent well over five minutes ensuring the small audience of regional policy makers, strategists, and consultants in the capital region that we do not oppose statistics or measurement as a practice. It should be self-evident, yet, as we present our critical take on what we call the politics of numbers, it seems hard to digest. Now, looking at the audience getting ready for questions after the presentation, we feel this tension again. There is frustration in the air. Some even seem angry, or at least annoyed.

So, the first question is asked. It is balanced, reasonable, and good. Like most of them are. But thematically it starts to add up. Towards the end frustration dominates. What do we actually mean when we argue that numbers are political? Isn't it actually we who are being political and ideological? And even more suspicious, a few times we have said that truth and objectivity are problematic concepts. Surely, we must agree that there are facts and that numbers have a particular quality that makes them good for communicating and portraying such facts? Numbers don't lie and, as actually shown in numerous rankings, this is in fact the most innovative region in the country. And we all know it is, right? Just as the numbers also tell us. The discussion continues, and soon we both feel a bit up against the wall. Climate change? Can we agree on that? That it is real and measurable objectively?

Afterwards, in the car home, we talk about it a lot. In fact, we talk about it for hours. And we are used to talking about truth, objectivity, and about research as a practice ridden with power and politics like all other social relations. From our perspective, this is not strange at all. Yet, it is frustrating also for us. Like there is a distance that must be traversed before we can even expect to get our points across. We end our discussion in a more positive feeling though. Again, we are actually used to this. In a way, that people become upset as we point out the political nature of measurement like they did tonight speaks precisely to the political dimension of numbers. Our talk at least spurred discussions on what particular kind of measures that may pass as political and what may not. People were engaged in political discussions. Examples were given. Questions were answered in ways that generated more questions.

A week later and we are giving the same presentation in another region. It is morning when we arrive at the office building where we are supposed to hold the seminar. We are greeted by our hosts and we do some small talk on our way through the corridors. Just as we are about to walk in to the seminar room, a woman, who is going to be one of the attendees, also arrives. She stops, introduces herself and shakes our hands before we walk in together. "It's going to be so great to listen to you today. People are really excited to talk to you. There was a new ranking in the paper yesterday. Did you see it? If not, welcome to the worst region of the country to live in!" She smiles and then adds: "We are so used to it now. We know how it works. Those rankings are designed in ways that makes it impossible for anyone other than the capital or old university regions to win. They really don't tell us anything." We have a short laugh together, and then we get into our presentation. We feel it already, and we say it out loud. This presentation is going to be different than the one the previous week. Perhaps this time we will have to defend the practice of measurement and the use of numbers in the first place. Because after all, they are important tools, right? Or what are we actually saying here? Again, afterwards, we debrief. And it takes some time. Then we decide to leave it precisely where we started this research years ago. Numbers are not only political. They are important governmental technologies. Instruments of governing that do things to the world in which they are articulated. Good things. Bad things. Therefore, it is crucial to understand their operations.

Who's the best and how can we learn to be the best?

Perhaps we can view them as insights into the struggle. As reports from the frontiers. In newspapers, in magazines, in government reports, and in everyday conversations we frequently encounter the reproduction of rankings, indices, comparisons, and league tables for cities, regions, and countries concerning a wide range of measures. As such, governmental technologies like these are deployed for many reasons; however, they are always intrinsically tied to the rationalities that govern the assemblage in which they are being articulated. In this chapter, we study the production of a particular kind of technologies that we refer to as *numerical devices*. In the context of what we are dealing with here, they are often instated in order to provide clear-cut answers to questions such as: Which city is the best to live in? What regions are the most innovative in the EU? Where can we find the most creative people? However, they also provide answers to the opposite questions. Which city is the worst to live in? What regions are the least innovative (and hence most backwards) in the EU? What regions are inhabited by really non-creative people?

This situation sometimes spurs discussions, like in the examples of the vignette above; however, most of the time, these technologies are particularly useful for promoting what is perceived to be 'objective' and 'unbiased' facts or knowledge. This quality is linked precisely to the fact that they build on numbers and numerical derivatives for portraying their message. We will get back to the question of objectivity later on; however, for now it is enough to say that regardless of the epistemic quality of numerical devices they inevitably 'do something' to the context in which they are articulated. In this sense, therefore, they are performative (Barad, 2007; Butler, 1990, 1993; Glass & Rose-Redwood, 2014; Mol, 2002). This chapter is ultimately about the performative aspects of numerical devices and how this, in turn, is linked to expertise. Moreover, much of their performativity lies in the almost intrinsic processes of comparison and commensuration that accompanies the creation of a new index or another form of numerical device. In this sense, they often constitute the basis for benchmarking procedures and, therefore, in this chapter we also provide examples that expand on this wider context of comparison among regions.

Regional development is a field permeated by these practices of measurement. To be fair, that could probably be said about most policy fields today, and as such the practices and technologies of measuring, gauging, ranking, and comparing are central for understanding the conditions that allow for the reproduction of certain forms of expertise in policy making more generally. As we will present in more detail below, in regional development, the most common and important measures that are being produced are generally in line with the master rationality of competitiveness. Indeed, we argue that the formulation of certain numerical devices is very much fundamental for the reproduction of competitiveness as a rationality in the first place. Moreover, these formulations are almost exclusively the domain of expertise. In other words, the specific form of governmental technologies that we opt to call numerical devices not only sustains a rationality through which expertise can be realized in a certain way, they are also good examples of concrete and hands on articulations of expertise in this field.

As indicated in the previous chapter, under the label *the rationality of intelligence* we gathered a number of associated principles that underscore the importance of measuring and comparing in contemporary regional development; however, we also pointed to the fact that the purpose of this rationality often is about learning. In this way, it ties into *the rationality of the strategos* and *the rationality of triage* as regions strive to use their intelligence gathering as means to learn, adapt, and become more successful in achieving higher levels of competitiveness. For this reason, we argue that the selective illustration of important governmental technologies that help foster traveling expertise should also include some aspects of this learning. Thus, as we go ahead and discuss and exemplify numerical devices as governmental technologies we continuously try to show how they connect to this intelligence gathering in the name of learning. In addition, as mentioned, we also make sure to showcase how practices of benchmarking and learning in a wider sense are comprised of additional elements beyond numerical devices.

So, for the purpose of this chapter we have chosen to illustrate how numerical devices operate as governmental technologies and how they are linked to the assemblage of traveling expertise. We consider how such devices are processed as part of regional development and also illustrate how they help bestow policy publications with a form of science modality. To be sure, this is far from an exhaustive selection of governmental technologies connected to the presence and sustenance of expertise in regional development; however, we do think they are important in terms of how they connect to the rationalities discussed in Chapter 3. As before, we draw on research conducted over the last decade and this means that we provide empirical examples and discussions from different sources. Specifically, our goal is precisely to *illustrate* salient expressions of the technologies. It is not to assess them in terms of impact, influence or quality.

More precisely then, what follows in this chapter is a two-part structure. In the first part, we introduce our take on numerical devices as we begin by activating some of the important scholarly works that have been published on the politics of numbers and the sociology of quantification over the past decades. This is then accompanied by an illustrative discussion on certain numerical devices in regional development that we have encountered in our research. In the second part, we broaden the discussion a bit as we turn to illustrations of how numerical devices are represented and communicated in policy. As we do so we also consider multimodal representations of expertise in regional development in a more general sense. This is done by using visual examples from the glossy forms of policy documents that are readily used throughout regional development today. In this context we also make some brief illustrations of what we call regional development for the children, where we base the illustrations on the resources that the EU uses to promote the importance of competitiveness to children and school teachers. The chapter then concludes by drawing the discussions together as we consider the relationship between the technologies presented here and traveling expertise.

Measurement, politics of large numbers, and regional development

In order to start the discussion of how numerical devices are constituted, how they manifest in regional development, and how they are linked to expertise, we need to begin with a recognition of the role of such devices in politics more generally. In what has now become a standard work with regards to the development of official and national statistical reasoning, Alain Desrosières (2014) argues that the intricate relationship between this institutional development and the evolution of statistics as an independent academic discipline involves an ongoing tension. It can be stated rather simply by asking the following question: do statistical measures simply represent an external reality or are they complicit in the construction of this reality? To be clear, this tension runs in multiple directions and crosses many boundaries, and it is not a simple matter of, for instance, academic statisticians claiming one thing while state bureaucrats and politicians claiming another. Rather, as national statistical bureaus were being set up during the eighteenth and nineteenth centuries they naturally started to generate and collect data. While some of these processes were fairly straightforward, collectively they fed into theoretical debates concerning, among other things, the development of probability theory (see also Hacking, 2006). Briefly put, how one views probability matters for the wider debate concerning if statistics in the hands of the state apparatus should be considered a descriptive or prescriptive exercise. Here, the take away point for us is the fact that what statistics is and what we can do with statistics has in many ways been an open-ended question since its inception, both as a state practice and as

a disciple within academia. In this book, we follow what we think is a com-
pelling strand of literature that emphasizes how numbers and statistics are part
of the ongoing social construction of reality. Moreover, we follow Desrosières
(2014) in his recommendation to pay attention to the processes of objectifica-
tion, or in other words how, in the processes of governing, certain elements are
created precisely with the ambition to *make things that hold* for the purpose of
discussion and policy deployment. This brings our point of departure closely in
line with the questions that we find most important in this regard, namely how
numbers and statistics are a vital part of politics and government.

Governing by numbers

What some authors have called 'governing by numbers' (Rose, 1991) and
'the politics of numbers' (Alonso & Starr, 1987; Desrosiéres, 2014) has been a
central concern of social scientists for a long time, perhaps particularly so for
those interested in governmentality. Indeed, in Foucault's original works the
theme of calculating, measuring, and in this way knowing the population, was
an important and recurrent theme as he charted the changing modes of rule
and started to investigate biopolitics more thoroughly (Foucault, 2007, 2008).
During the nineteenth century, several states throughout Europe and beyond
had established central agencies for the collection and publication of census
data in which the population was not only counted but also measured according to a number of different parameters. Indeed, this governing through numbers was, according to Foucault, an important part of the emergence of liberal
governmentality and it constituted a vital part of the inception of biopolitics
in the ruling of nations (Elden, 2007; Foucault, 2007, 2008; Hacking, 1991).

Today, governing is more or less unthinkable without numbers and we are
enmeshed within such an avalanche of figures that we seldom pay attention to
the considerable amount of governmental work that goes into the production
of even the most mundane calculus of everyday life. Consider for instance the
basic practice of keeping records of where people in a given state or region
live so that it is possible to calculate the population of counties and cities. This
requires a machinery of highly educated civil servants, computer systems,
data bases, laws, and indeed also complex systems of dividing territories into
properties, houses, streets, and boroughs, to name but a few things. Moreover
these rather basic numbers also have profound effects in most states since they
constitute not only a measure of the number of people that live in a particular
place, they often also function as the basis for taxation and (re)distribution
of public funds and they are generally the base for the democratic system in
terms of election procedures. Thus, as argued by Nicholas Rose (1991:676):

> [...] such numbers do not merely inscribe a pre-existing reality. They
> constitute it. Techniques of inscription and accumulation of facts about
> "the population", the "national economy", "poverty" render visible a
> domain with a certain internal homogeneity and external boundaries. In

each case the collection and aggregation of numbers participates in the fabrication of a "clearing" within which thought and action can occur. Numbers here delineate "fictive spaces" for the operation of government, and establish a "plane of reality", marked out by a grid of norms, on which government can operate.

Thus, numbers and calculative techniques are examples of governmental technologies that operate intertwined with political rationalities as a particular domain is being instated as a governable terrain. They help relay the rationale, and they are vital for providing an infrastructure for action on behalf of government; however, as pointed out by Rose in the quote above, they are also very much shaping the object that is to be governed. So much that they often become the object. For example, innovation may be an empty signifier that can be understood as many things but after inscribing it in terms of numbers and indicators those will affect what innovation really is, whether this is the goal or not. Similarly, competitiveness among regions must be made through governing. It needs to be established as a 'thing,' and one of the most powerful ways of doing so is through numbers and numerical devices. Indeed, as we have argued for above, for competitiveness it seems more or less necessary to have a measure that can be used to gauge the performance of different units as they square off against each other. Taken together then, in the governmentality literature there is a quite explicit recognition of how numbers and numerical devices are part and parcel of the practices involved as a particular object or domain is being rendered governable. That being said, we argue that other scholarly fields and positions have developed a more thorough understanding of the particular effects of numbers and quantitative reasoning in society. Hence, we propose that by paying attention to some of the findings in sociology and science and technology studies (STS) we can fashion a better understanding of how numbers can be assembled into numerical devices that then may be put to work as governmental technologies.

A sociology of quantification

The effect of numbers and quantification throughout society has been studied in the literature that is sometimes called 'sociology of quantification' (cf. Krause Hansen, 2015; Krause Hansen & Flyverbom, 2015; Krause Hansen & Porter, 2012; Nelson Espeland & Sauders, 2007; Nelson Espeland & Stevens, 2008; Porter, 2012), and often, these works extend into STS, building in particular on the insights offered by actor-network theory (eg. Callon, 1998; Latour, 1987, 2005; Law & Mol, 2002; Mol, 2002). While it would be possible to delve into a number of topics in this literature, here we limit ourselves to some basic theorization concerning effects of numbers as they become part of governing.

When numbers are mobilized as part of governing their role and function can broadly be separated into two main categories. First, they fill the function of *marking* and second, they *commensurate* (Nelson Espeland & Stevens, 2008). Before discussing the difference between these functions some clarification is needed. So far the terms numbers, quantification, indices, rankings, and other forms of calculative techniques have been used more or less interchangeably; however, it makes sense to distinguish between numbers and numerical devices. Thus, as we coin this term, *numerical devices*, we consider it to designate a composition of numbers, merged together with either other numbers (as in composite indices) or other modalities of representation (such as graphical representations in charts, diagrams or tables). In other words, numbers are the building blocks of numerical devices such as indices and rankings, and while such devices inherit the governing properties of numbers, they also add to them.

So, returning to the marking function of numbers, this fills the basic role of categorical representation that is similar to some everyday function of words. For instance, we use numbers to distinguish houses from each other along a certain street, or we may think of telephone numbers, postal codes, bank account numbers, ip addresses or the numbers on the jerseys of a sports team to understand that these kinds of labeling and marking are more or less unavoidable parts of most formally organized societies. These may seem simple, however, there are many such classificatory numerical devices that are great governing achievements in themselves. To begin with, all measurement basically starts out with definitions, taxonomies, and categorization that must be brokered among parties and agreed upon by political interests. As an example of this, we will consider the ambitious program set up by the UN to work towards sustainable development. Recently, this initiative is starting to be explicitly incorporated into regional development strategies around Europe, and thus it is likely to be important in the years to come, not only for national and supranational governing bodies, but also for regional ones.

The UN sustainable development program is part of the so called 2030 agenda and is explicitly designed to help governments around the world transform into a sustainable future. To this end, the program breaks down sustainable development into 17 distinct areas that are further divided into target goals and a set of indicators related to each role. To repeat then, this is an example of the *marking* function of numbers. Even before numbers can be generated and collected, what they represent must be part of particular taxonomies. In the case of the UN sustainable development goals, this means that significant governing efforts have been made to reach a consensus where the 17 different areas have been agreed upon and then made translatable into categorical representation that can be expressed for all nations. So, taking just one of the goals as an example, say goal number five – gender equality, this breaks down into nine different targets, each with a set number of indicators for gauging the progression of that target. Thus, target 5.5 reads:

> Ensure women's full and effective participation and equal opportunities for leadership at all levels of decision-making in political, economic and public life

To measure this target two indicators are used:
5.5.1 Proportion of seats held by women in national parliaments and local
      governments
5.5.2 Proportion of women in managerial positions

(13)

To underline what may be fairly obvious, this form of operationalization, as all like it, is not perfect. One can imagine the discussions, differences, and struggles that led to this target and its indicators. In addition, the different positions were probably restricted in their conceptions and definitions by the forms of data that are possible to generate in meaningful ways across all nations. Simply put, there is no neutral position as to what constitutes gender equality. This is an inherently political dimension and while numbers in the end may do a good work of portraying transparency and objectivity, they are as grounded in the political as other forms of language. While this highlights the political dimension of any marking practices associated with numbers, the main achievement here in terms of governing is that the end result is an impressive and comprehensive system of categorization upon which rule can be enacted. Remember that the example above represents just one target under one area. Taking into account all of the 17 areas with each set of targets and corresponding indicators reveals a complex array of political decisions that have been crystallized into categories that now are waiting to be filled with data. Indeed, after the dust has settled, so to speak, the political dimensions of marking tend to disappear (cf. Öjehag-Pettersson, 2019) and instead we are left with precise measures, glossy diagrams, tables, and website dashboards where people interactively are able to produce comparisons and infographics. Throughout this process the marking has resulted in a precise language for what gender equality is. It has allowed the passing of information and comparison over huge distances in a format that is flexible and robust in ways that words are not.

While the UN example illustrates how the markings of numerical devices make possible a very precise form of categorization that is hard to replicate with words, it also illustrates what Vaughn Higgins and Wendy Larner (2010:205) have called standardizing work. Rather than focusing on standardization, 'which implies a process that is complete, successful, and black-boxed' they view standardizing work 'as an ongoing and never completed process of "making up" objects, subjects, and practices of modern governing.' This, again, underlines how the UN sustainability goals, and similar numerical devices, should not be taken for granted and treated as residual parts of governing a particular domain. On the contrary, their existence should be considered important, if not fundamental, for understanding this governing. So, the standardizing of everything from shipping containers to disease classification to goals and targets for sustainability signals considerable amount of governing work in the processes, which leads up to the actual deployment of the standards. Furthermore, while numbers do offer some aspects of classification that words do not, they have just as much an effect of 'making up people' (Hacking, 2006) as all forms of discourse and in this sense what they offer, despite their precise, additive, and combinable nature, is not more transparency, but rather the illusion of it — a phenomenon that has been debated for a long time in the philosophy of science (Hansen, 2015). Therefore, recognizing the marking capacity of numbers is a way of pointing to the fact that numerical devices, like 'speech acts' (Austin, 1976), do something to the context in which they are articulated. They are not exact representations of reality and neutral ways of classifying and grouping social phenomena.

In terms of standardizing work, numerical devices are often looked to not only because they offer an illusion of transparency and their, in certain ways, more precise register than words, but rather they also represent the first step in *commensuration*. For Nelson Espeland and Stevens (2008:408) commensuration entails 'the valuation or measuring of different objects with a common metric' and thus, by marking with numbers it becomes possible to 'transform all difference into quantity' uniting 'objects by encompassing them under a shared cognitive system.' Hence, prices on goods, standardized tests, and the rising number of indices and rankings in social and political life, not least in urban and regional development, are examples of commensuration processes. They have a capacity to 'reduce, simplify, and integrate information' (Nelson Espeland & Sauder, 2007:16) while simultaneously also marking out difference precisely through this unification as it makes it possible to distinguish between, for instance, a region with high levels of innovation and one with low levels. In such a case, commensuration in the form of indices and rankings reduces all the possible forms of difference in terms of innovation in different regions to a single measure. In other words, numerical devices that commensurate help decontextualize and make the phenomenon that is measured more mobile, which contributes to the often authoritative position of numbers in governance (Krause Hansen, 2015; Krause Hansen & Flyverbom, 2015; Nelson Espeland & Stevens, 2008).

In the context of regional development, we have an abundance of this kind of indices and rankings that can help illustrate how commensuration works, from local examples to supranational initiatives organized and maintained by, for instance, the OECD and the EU. Here we draw on the so called Regional Wellbeing Index developed by OECD, not because this is more important than all other numerical devices in regional development, but rather because it is a good illustration of contemporary trends in this regard. In particular, it is interactive and visually appealing as it appears in the web tool designed for people to compare and contrast – or in other words, initiate commensuration processes.

First of all, the work with regional development at the OECD is illustrative in itself of the rationalities we presented in Chapter 3. They state their policy as this:

> OECD work on regional development recognizes that a new approach to regional development is emerging; one that promises more effective use of public resources and significantly better policy outcomes. This involves a

shift away from redistribution and subsidies for lagging regions in favor of measures to increase the competitiveness of all regions.

(14)

Hence, the regional wellbeing index fits firmly within this framework; however, it is also an explicit attempt to move away from one sided and simple measures of competitiveness or wellbeing, such as regional GDP or other economic measures:

> There is a growing awareness that we must go beyond GDP and economic statistics to get a fuller understanding of how society is doing. But it is also crucial to zoom in on how life is lived. Where you live have an impact on your quality of life, and in return, you contribute to making your community a better place. Comparable measures of regional well-being offer a new way to gauge what policies work and can empower a community to act to achieve higher well-being for its citizens.
>
> (15)

So, like the aforementioned example of the UN sustainable development goals and targets, the Wellbeing index also starts with classifications and groupings of variables. Indeed, the numerical device is actually not just one composite index, rather it is a tool that measures regions and assigns them scores between 0 and 10 at 11 different scales representing different dimensions of wellbeing. A high score indicates that a region is performing well relative to other regions. Again, like the UN example, each of the 11 dimensions (or topics as they are officially called) are captured using a range of indicators that then are weighted together to provide a score that is comparable across OECD regions. Like many other tools of this kind, the articulated purpose is benchmarking for the sake of learning. Rather than to just produce rankings where we can observe current winners and losers, the OECD encourages users of their website to utilize the tool that they provide in order to develop their regions in the areas where they are lacking relative to others.

In many ways, the web tool, as illustrated in Figure 4.1 below, represents the latest horizon for the operation of numerical devices as it places the complex calculations and comparisons directly in the hands of the user (although this also introduces carefully calculated restrictions in the name of governing). In this case, it allows a user to select a starting region from a map depicting all OECD regions across the globe. After doing so the website quickly loads up a profile for the selected region with a figure visually representing the 11 different dimensions of wellbeing and the corresponding scores. Moreover, it shows detailed information for each score in a set of color coded panels where the score for the particular dimensions is broken down into indicators. In this process, the system also shows how the selected region ranks in comparison to other regions in its country as well as the rest of the OECD. Finally, it also suggests a group of regions with similar profiles as the selected one. In this way, the user can easily navigate to more detailed comparisons. In other words, this is a versatile

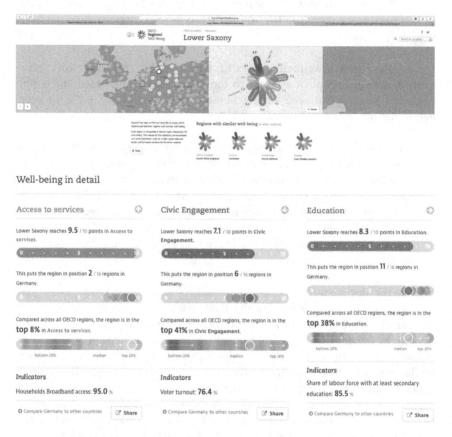

Figure 4.1 Regional well-being index, panel examples (Lower Saxony, Germany). The images in this figure are reproduced screenshots from the website of the regional well-being index, developed by the OECD (15).

tool that marks and commensurates the notion of wellbeing and even though the purpose is not the ranking *per se*, this seems to be a more or less inevitable part of commensuration processes (cf. Öjehag-Pettersson, 2019). This brings us back to the effect of numbers as they are assembled into numerical devices.

From marking and commensuration to reactivity and performativity

In sum, marking and commensuration can be understood as two ends of a spectrum for the functions of numerical devices when they are mobilized as governmental technologies. On the one hand, the marking function is always required for commensuration, and on the other hand few devices exist exclusively for marking, but rather, like the UN sustainability goals and the OECD wellbeing index, they are a platform for commensuration.

As mentioned, the combination of marking and commensuration inscribes the numerical devices with a number of qualities as governmental technologies that, in certain ways, make them different from words and written text. While this is not a distinct demarcation line, research has pointed to at least four such general qualities (Hansen & Porter, 2012; Krause Hansen, 2015). First, numerical devices can be said to be highly mobile. This is a function of the commensuration that decontextualizes and thus makes the device possible to be transported and installed in a wide array of settings. In principle, an index that originally was developed in an English context could easily be exported to other spaces far beyond the context where it originated. Second, and tied to this, numbers are stable constructs in the sense that $5 + 5 = 10$, regardless of setting. This make them good for communicating messages in ways that are easy to decode and understand, which adds even more to their recognition as authoritative and reliable. Third, while numbers are stable, they are also very combinable. This means that a particular indicator developed for one purpose may easily be inserted as part of more complex calculations for other purposes. For example, it is not uncommon to find indices that are themselves constituted by a combination of other indices. Finally, numerical devices are particularly well suited for ordering. Indeed, this is often the articulated purpose for this kind of governmental technologies so that the marking and commensuration aspects are simply necessary steps that must be taken before the important part begins.

For the purpose of this chapter it makes sense to discuss this ordering function a little further. While all numbers as governmental technologies 'do' something in terms of marking and commensuration, and while they all have the properties of mobility, stability, and combinability the ordering function of numerical devices makes them reactive (Nelson Espeland & Sauder, 2007; Nelson Espeland & Stevens, 2008), or using a term and concept more at home in the governmentality literature, they have properties that make them performative (c.f Butler, 1990; Callon, 1998). To understand this effect, we may begin by discussing the notion of reactivity before articulating our preferred concept of performativity.

The concept of reactivity is generally viewed as a methodological problem within positivist social science since it denotes the (unavoidable) fact that the research performed by social scientists may affect the phenomenon they study, particularly when they study humans. Thus, a goal then becomes to minimize reactivity so that the results generated in, say, a study of employees at a university through the means of surveys are not 'contaminated' by the fact that the employees know that they are being studied and therefore provide answers that they otherwise would have not. In this way, the concept of reactivity is useful for understanding what happens when numerical devices are put to work as governmental technologies. Since they have a very profound ordering and ranking capacity one almost immediate effect is that the object of study will react based on the fact that they are being rated and ordered. This reactivity effect is detailed by Nelson Espeland and Sauder

(2007) in their studies on the effect of ranking systems for United States law schools and universities. In addition to discussing marking and commensuration, they also illustrate how reactivity manifests in this case as self-fulfilling prophecies directly related to the practice of ranking schools. While the particular index that they study do provide a 'raw score' for all the universities that have law schools across the US, the ranking positions tend to be what external audiences remember and magnify. Since 40 percent of the scores in this highly influential index is based on the reputation of the schools the rankings produce a looping effect so that students and faculty members themselves rely on the rankings when they asses the general quality of their school. In this way, the artificial lines that are drawn between what is identified as 'the top tier' institutions and the rest generally take on a quality of being real differences rather than condensed and simplified measures. While this may be a methodological problem, it also illustrates some general properties of numerical devices as governmental technologies. In addition to the looping effects of self-fulfilling prophecies Nelson Espeland and Sauder (2007) show how universities start to react to the measures as their revenues depend on it. Therefore, deans at the law schools often try to manipulate and construct aspects of their school that may directly affect their ranking position. Since the index has become so established as a measuring device of quality, the deans feel that bad positions are immediately held against them in the competition for funding both internally within their university as well as externally. This effect is most pronounced among the universities that are not considered 'top tier' as they are continuously questioned by various boards and management systems that, based on the ranking positions, urge them to make significant changes in the school programs even though faculty and students may feel that they are doing well.

As mentioned, instead of speaking of reactivity, which in certain ways reflect a more rationalist position on the effects of numbers and statistics than the position we hold, we prefer the term and concept of performativity to describe effects of governing akin to what Espeland and Sauder (2007) capture under reactivity. As we do so we follow the tradition emanating from Judith Butler's (eg. 1993) work as the concept has been picked up and further developed in feminist theory (eg. Barad, 2007) as well as in STS (for an overview of the concept see for instance Glass and Rose-Redwood, 2014). Thus, put short, for Butler (1993:20) performativity is 'the power of discourse to produce effects through reiteration' and while her prime example concerns the way that bodies are gendered through iterative practices, the notion has been picked up and contributed to theoretical development in academic fields far beyond gender studies. This means that when we speak of numerical devices as performative, we recognize that they are not mere reflections of the world that surrounds them. Rather, numerical devices act upon the world, regardless of the intention behind them. Indeed, they order, structure and intervene in this world as a function of them coming into being, so to speak. Thus, the performative aspect of numerical devices, or any other governmental technology for that matter, lies precisely in the fact that they actually do something to the world.

While often described as neutral and objective reflections of a particular social field that enable conscious actions from the rulers in one direction or the other, they are already guiding action as they are formulated.

For this reason, we argue, a growing body of research concerning the increased tendency to use rankings, ratings, and other forms of what we call numerical devices throughout the social world has started to recognize that perhaps the most important questions in this regard are not primarily about the lack of reliability and validity of the devices. Rather, as argued by Esposito and Stark (2019), the very reason that rankings and ratings are increasingly important in everything from restaurant guides to competitiveness tables is that even though they simplify, obscure, fail to predict, and are subjective, they provide orientation in the world. It should be clear by now, that for us, this orientation is not neutral. It was always already an act of governing in its articulation, influenced by certain dominating political rationalities.

Empirical illustrations

To bring this discussion back to the context of regional development, consider the following brief example. The organization NORDREGIO is a research center focused on regional development in the Nordic countries and the EU. It publishes a range of reports as well as a peer-reviewed journal. Part of their work is an index called 'Regional Potential Index.' NORDREGIO describes it like this:

> Nordregio's Regional Potential Index is constructed around a series of key socio-economic indicators with relevance in an analysis of regional development. The data from the nine selected indicators is categorized into three dimensions: demographic, labor force and economic.
>
> (17)

As such, it is a typical numerical device as discussed above. This means that it has a capacity to commensurate through simplification while still maintaining a quality of transparency and objectivity regardless of the political assumptions that underpins it. Importantly, we are not concerned here with the research undertaken by NORDREGIO as they construct the index; however, we are interested in how this research is picked up and communicated. Thus, this index is interesting in terms of how its results travel. While the intention of NORDREGIO might simply be to describe and accurately gauge what they identify as regional potential across the 74 different regions of the Nordic countries, the numerical device itself immediately have governing effects in terms of commensuration and comparison. Indeed, one of its main outlets is a publication and communications platform issued by the Nordic Council of Ministers (NCM) called 'State of the Nordic Region 2018' where the results are communicated in the form of a written report as well as a website and social media such as a YouTube film. In this context, the focus is on the highs and the lows of the index and there are a few surprises. Capital regions dominate and have much higher scores than most rural regions and Stockholm, Sweden, is crowned the most dynamic region of the Nordic. By simple deduction then, life in Stockholm is much more dynamic than in many peripheral regions that it outscores by a factor of three in terms of index points. Conversely, put in simplified terms, life in most Nordic regions outside of the capitals hold significantly less potential.

This result is not lost on policy makers and media as the numerical device is communicated. So, the largest paper in Sweden, *Dagens Nyheter* writes a piece on the results of the index after NCM releases its latest (2018) report and in this the focus is on 'climbers' and particularly how Stockholm now is the highest ranked region in the Nordic as opposed to how it was only the third highest ranked in the previous iteration of the index. In the article, a top ten table is presented and the results are generally identified as evidence for high levels of competitiveness, not only in these ten regions but also for most urban areas in the Nordic. In a typical way, the article also reports how Gävleborg is the region in Sweden with lowest potential. Several regions around the countries held seminars or workshops where regional policy makers and analysts sat down to analyze and discuss the position and 'movement' of their respective regions on the index league tables. While these talks seemed to be about learning, they also seem to have departed from notions of winners and losers in terms of index scores. Similarly, the Swedish government issued a press release and they too focused on the rankings and competition aspects that the index enables. Foreign Minister Margot Wallström underlined this at a press conference:

> The Nordic countries are like a small family and like it usually is in all families we like to compete a bit. This is why I am particularly proud to announce the winner in the Nordregio Regional Potential Index, namely Stockholm.
>
> (18)

Taken together, the governing practices that arise around this numerical device are typical in terms of what we discussed above. In particular, the fact that what is often communicated to be a descriptive learning tool inevitably turns into discussions of ranking and best practice. Indeed, the brief illustrations of how the Regional Potentials Index travels is not particularly aligned with the ambition that Nordregio articulates:

> The purpose of Nordregio's Regional Potential Index is to show the current performance of the 74 administrative regions of the Nordic countries; to identify regions with high potential for future development and their common denominators; and to identify regions in need of further support and policy measures to strengthen their potential and meet existing challenges. Last but not least, the index provides policy-makers with insights on regional strengths and weaknesses, and could be used for comparative learning between Nordic regions with similar geographies

but different outcomes in the ranking when it comes to creating effective regional development strategies.

(19)

Again, the index becomes a numerical device that not only is wrapped up in current rationalities of regional development with their focus on competitiveness, we argue that it also helps enable and foster this rationality, even if it would be designed with other purposes in mind. Indeed, numerical devices are enlisted as benchmarking tools in more or less all forms of governing and one important effect of this is what may be understood as an elitist emphasis. There is always the 'best practice' example that all others are supposed to follow and often this example is a new inscription of already established power orders. Moreover, as Isabelle Bruno (2009) has shown concerning the Open Method of Coordination (OMC) initiated by the EU, the benchmarking targets that are facilitated by the numerical devices are always moving, making them particularly adept at promoting a never-ending chase for competitiveness. These moving targets turn competitiveness through benchmarking into an indefinite discipline, a process under which policy makers are relentlessly compelled to asses themselves in order to improve according to the benchmarks. As put by Bruno (2009:278):

> Indeed, benchmarking helps decision makers to reach consensus by translating political problems of collective action into statistical issues of quantification. This way of coordinating Member States tends to Europeanize national policies through comparable figures rather than integrate them by supranational law. These statistical figures do not reveal a measurable degree of competitiveness which pre-exists the actual process of its measurement. They create the conditions for competition and make competitive relations possible, thereby shaping the EU in a specific way. It is in that sense that the OMC effectively contributes to the emergence of a "competitive Europe" which entails not just competition with Japan and the United States, but also within Europe between nations, turning them into performing and competing bodies, instead of collaborative members of a union.

In sum, then, by providing the theoretical discussion and the empirical illustrations above, our goal has been to showcase how a certain set of governmental technologies and numerical devices operate in regional development. It is our position that these tools are both an expression of expertise while at the same time also being some of the more prominent vehicles for expertise to be present in the first place. Before we go on to elaborate on this, we will shift the attention a bit. Following the articulation of the numerical devices quickly reveals another prominent feature of their part of policy, namely the way they are (re)presented. By this we mean that numerical devices are used alongside standard written text in ways that change the modalities through which contemporary policy, in regional development as well as in other areas, is communicated.

Representing expertise: multimodality, comic policy, and regional development for the children

A striking feature of many policy documents, at least in the context of urban and regional development, is how they often contain ample amount of graphical representations, and certainly not only of numerical devices. In fact, these documents are often filled with typographically appealing layout, figures, photos, diagrams, and artistic sketches that make them resemble advertising brochures. In this way, some of the most important documents in regional development are *multimodal*. We use this term to designate texts that contain forms of semiotic modalities other than the standard written alphabet. Thus, a document containing written text and graphical representations of a numerical device, or a table presenting information based on that numerical device in a specific way, would be an example of a multimodal text. As a growing body of scholarly works have shown, there are semiotic connotations associated with such multimodal texts that go beyond what we have so far said to be important for numerical devices (for influential overviews see Kress & Van Leeuwen, 2006; Rose, 2016). Therefore, in this final part of the chapter we will spend some time detailing what we think are important multimodal effects that arise as numerical devices are represented graphically or in any other modality as part of a broader text. Moreover, we will also expand on the notion of multimodal policy documents and consider them as an important class of governmental technologies of their own. Indeed, we argue that the way policy documentation is produced in regional development through multiple modalities (documents, films, games, maps, and websites) is important for understanding how expertise is enabled and expressed within the assemblage. We do this by mobilizing two different thematic examples of multimodality here. First, we continue the discussion on numerical devices and focus on some of the implications accompanying them as they are graphically represented in policy documents. Second, we expand on other aspects of multimodality to consider the advertisement-like qualities that many policy documents have nowadays. As we do so, we also highlight how the EU, as part of their ambition to teach kids about regional development, have started to use comics, films, and games to teach about the benefits of innovation and entrepreneurship.

Before we go ahead to use our empirical illustrations in this regard, however, it is first necessary to mention how what we present here can only be a brief overview. While we do offer some semiotic analysis and interpretations of the examples, our main focus here is, as in the rest of the chapter, to illustrate how multimodal policy documents operate as governmental technologies in relation to our notion of traveling expertise. Hence, the purpose of the following sections is not to fully exhaust images, videos, and multimodality in terms of what Rose (2016) calls visual methodologies. While this would certainly be interesting, it is a topic wide enough for a book of its own. That being said, we do wish to stress how in the assemblage of regional development it seems crucial to consider the prevalence of multimodal policy documents and platforms.

Numerical devices and multimodality

As we consider the multimodal features of numerical devices when they are made part of policy documents, we will use a local example of such a device. In a way the prevalence and existence of these local takes on numerical devices is also part of a global phenomenon. They arise from the fact that while global performance indicators have grown in prominence over the last decades (Erkkilä & Piironen, 2014; Giannone, 2017), such devices are often not fine-tuned enough to provide measures at scales appropriate for all regions in all countries. Thus, it is common to find numerical devices developed and produced by local expertise to fulfill a perceived need to measure, for instance, entrepreneurial ambitions in all French regions. For our purpose we use an index developed in Sweden by the collaboration arena Reglab together with the consultancy firm Kontigo. This index, simply called the innovation index, attempts to gauge the innovative capacity of all 21 Swedish regions. As mentioned, Reglab is an arena for collaboration among Swedish regions, agencies, and firms involved with regional development in the country. This means that, as an organization, it is funded by its members (the regions and agencies) and works with a wide range of projects to facilitate learning among the regions. The innovation index is one such learning project and to this date it has been updated three times since it was first published in 2011. Like in the illustrations discussed above, while the index was intended primarily as a learning tool, regions quickly started to draw on it for the purpose of measuring their relative performance and to identify how to catch up with respect to other regions. Interestingly, in many cases it has been made part of the so called Regional Development Strategies (RDS) that Swedish regions are required by the state to produce and follow up. Since all regions publish their RDS and related documents such as Regional Innovation Strategies, they are readily available and thus a suitable material for a discussion on the way that numerical devices add, shift or alter modalities of such documents.

Here, we will illustrate primarily two effects pertaining to rather common ways of representing numerical devices as part of a multimodal text composition. First, let us consider what the presence of a diagram, a graph or a table 'does' to a text in terms of modality in more general terms. Indeed, it can do a lot of things, however, in the context of policy documentation we argue that the primary reason for including graphical representations of a numerical device is to impose a form of 'science' or 'expertise' modality on the text. Graphs, figures, numbers, and abstract models belong to the domain of science and the expertise that comes along with it. Today, when there is a strong notion of evidence based policy, one way to bestow a policy program with some of the prestige, objectivity, and transparency, often associated with science, is to use one of its hallmark tools, namely numbers and numerical devices.

By including a diagram or a figure based on a numerical device within the arrangement of text, images, and typography that comprise a multimodal document, its producers are often able to place a modality marker in the document. This marker signals precisely the mentioned objectivity and transparency that academic publications are known for; however, it also deviates from these publications in important ways. Think about the way figures, diagrams, and tables are used in scientific publications. In those circumstances, they are often complex and abstract simplifications of a particular process or result. However, while they are abstract, the goal is also to make them precise. This leaves little room for layout and design to be considered in any other respect than to produce precision and abstraction of the process or result that the researcher wishes to convey. Often, in research journals in all disciplines, diagrams and figures are part and parcel of what we call *models* of any particular process or phenomenon. While the purpose and usage of such models vary, they are generally scrutinized hard in peer-review process in terms of how well they actually function as models for what the researcher is trying to describe. This often means that precision and clarity must accompany the graphical representations of the models as well as a purposeful description concerning the meaning of using this specific model in this circumstance.

To point out an obvious contrast in terms of how numerical devices can be represented visually, consider the way they are often used in media, particularly the tabloid press. Here, the precision and clarity is far less important than the story one is able to enhance, steer, and direct by including stylized figures and tables. Even in much more serious media outlets, the attention to visual appeal often stands in quite clear contrast to how the same data would have been presented graphically in an academic journal. Simply put, the way that the visual representations work differs with respect to the type of publication.

We argue, as mentioned earlier, that in the context of policy documents the primary function of introducing graphical representations of a numerical device is to place a modality marker of 'science.' Consider how the innovation index is used in a so-called Innovation program of a Swedish region in Figure 4.2. Notice, how this is a document filled with stylish layout, sketches, and that general advertisement look we mentioned before. However, when the innovation index is introduced, the style changes. Not only are the spider diagrams examples of when graphical representations of numerical devices provide a science modality, but the font and typography also change into more 'strict' styles. At the same time, looking more closely at the diagrams reveals very little in terms of detail and precision. Actual numbers are omitted and (in line with what we have said before concerning numerical devices) the general idea of the diagrams is to compare this region with the national average. There is no information on how the index has been assembled or how it has been calculated. Put short, the purpose here certainly is not to allow a reader to reproduce the index, develop it in certain ways or to apply it in other contexts. While such activities could have been the idea in an academic journal, it is not the point here. At the same time, the representation also does not resemble the often overt and rather 'in your face' kind of diagrams that

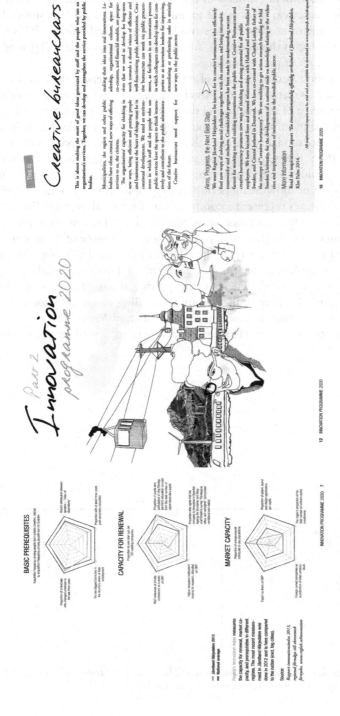

Figure 4.2 Numerical devices as modality markers. Reproduction of pages 7, 12, and 18 from the Innovation program of region Jämtland Härjedalen 2020 (20:7, 12, 18).

we would expect to find in the tabloid press. Instead, it is our interpretation that in policy documents, at least in those relating to regional development, the way that numerical devices are graphically represented falls somewhere in between standard academic ways and less precise media usage. This helps them tell a story with the diagrams, figures, and tables, while still giving the documents an aura of precise science.

One of the most common ways of representing numerical devices is to use basic charts, such as scatterplots and bar charts. We will use an example of this to show that the usage of such basic and simple representations has semiotic qualities that alter the meaning of its surrounding text. Not only do they help with installing a science modality but they also impose certain interpretations of data.

Consider then, the way that innovative capacity of regions as measured by the innovation index is represented in Figure 4.3. In its essence, this is a very typical variation of showcasing performance graphically where the individually plotted measures represent a combination of values along two dimensions for each unit of analysis (in this case Swedish regions). Here we will just make one main point, namely that such diagrams produce a sense of movement and direction out of what is actually separate and individual points of measure. This effect is also often present in line charts plotted over time and bar charts sorted with respect to frequency. In this particular case, the clear markings of the four quadrants help induce an understanding of linearity for the evolution of regions regarding their innovative capacity. While this may not be the intention, questions of 'where are we at' are transformed into questions of

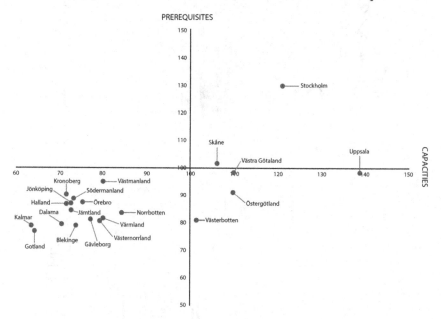

Figure 4.3 Semiotic qualities of basic charts. The chart is reproduced from the official Reglab documentation for the innovation index (21).

'where are we going' or 'where should we be.' Thus, in this case regions are represented as located on a continuum ranging from less evolved into more evolved ones. The diagram therefore gives any reader a general idea of what direction the less evolved regions will move if only they follow the best practice examples (Kress & van Leeuwen, 2006). In other words, this graphical representation enhances the commensuration enabled through the creation of the index in the first place, and at this point the fact that what we are seeing in the plot is actually a set of measures for discrete units of analysis is often long gone. While this is not the case in Figure 4.3, a common instance where this effect is at its most pronounced is when a linear regression trend line is superimposed upon the plot, or when such a line replaces the plot entirely.

There are many more ways in which graphical representations of numerical devices have modality effects, perhaps particularly when they are involved in the kind of modeling discussed above. In such cases, it is common to see components of indices represented as boxes together with external components (also often represented by some geometrical shape) and lines or arrows linking the different parts of the model together. Again, the way such models are presented in policy documents work along the same lines as discussed above in that they install a 'science' modality while still being quite opaque or imprecise. A particularly common way that such opaque features manifest is related to the lines and arrows in models. It is often very hard to tell what they mean exactly. That they signify a relationship between one or more elements of the model is usually the first interpretation that comes to mind; however, in policy documents the models are rarely explained like they would have been in scientific circumstances. Thus, to use a very general and abstract example, we often have no way of telling if two boxes tied together by an arrow signal causation or transformation. In the first case, we could read the representations as one of the boxes causing the emergence or existence of the other, whereas in the second case the arrow would stand for one box transforming into something else under specific circumstances.

Consider Figure 4.4 as an example of these abstract models in policy. This does not involve a direct modeling of a numerical device; however, the principles are the same. In addition, this kind of models is very common in urban- and regional development policy documents. In this particular case, the region at hand (Galicia, Spain) has modeled what they call its Innovation system and its existing relations. Now, to make things very clear, the purpose of using this example is certainly not to put the producers of this specific document in this particular region under critical scrutiny (there are many other examples of this from all regions in Europe). Rather, the point is to illustrate how a science modality often is instated in documents and how the purpose of such models in this context, while utilizing and portraying scientific means of graphical representation, hardly can be said to fill the same function as in a scientific publication. Again, just to balance things a bit, we are well aware that there are quite a few models published in scientific journals that certainly express the same kind of ambiguities and unclear graphical representations. However, while this is a methodological problem in academic circumstances,

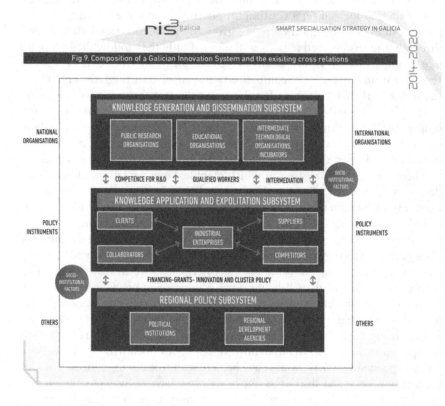

Figure 4.4 Abstract models and science modality in policy documents. Reproduction of page 41 from the RIS3 documentation of Galicia's Smart Specialization Strategy (22:41).

it is not automatically so in a policy context. Simply put, the purpose of using a model like this in a policy document was never to represent scientific argumentation in ways that simplify them or make them empirically testable for others. It was about the discourse surrounding evidence based policy making and the need for science modality in policy documentation as well as the legitimizing effects of expertise.

Multimodal policy documents and regional development for the children

Moving on from the science modality and the graphical representation of numerical devices in policy documents, we have mentioned several times by now that many key policy documents in regional development have started to resemble advertisement campaigns for certain brands. Indeed, branding and other means to communicate the attraction of a specific region is an important facet in the strive for competitiveness. Recall that the rationality of strategos works towards a particular form of governing where it is important to develop a region as a place where the right people want to live. In the following we will make three brief points about how this stylized multimodal presentation often takes shape in the major policy documents produced by regions in Europe.

First, while there are many important semiotic qualities that could be analyzed in this context, something that unites these documents is how they actually portray in images what an attractive region is and should be. While the policies draw on the local qualities in their respective regions there is a quite uniform way of displaying two main things, namely natural qualities of the region that we may call *amenities* and some form of *urban environment* that is connected to forms of global flows. In essence then, these representations enhance and direct statements made in written text about the need to be attractive for people and businesses in the sense that, as we detail in Chapters 3 and 5, it caters to a specific segment of the population. In Figure 4.5 we have reproduced what we find to be two typical expressions of this from a Danish regional development strategy.

Second, apart from the fact that the strategies and other forms of policy documents often portray a global idea of what an attractive region is, they generally also spend quite a lot of time depicting knowledge and innovations. Again, we argue that while the different regions draw on their local context there is a remarkable unity in terms of how knowledge is represented through images in the most important policy documents. Not only is it striking that

Figure 4.5 Multimodal representations of urban qualities and amenities. Reproduction of pages 30–31 and pages 48–49 in the regional development strategy of Region Syddanmark. Titles translate to 'Strong connections' in the urban image and 'Green possibilities' in the image of the child playing in the water (23:30–31, 48–49).

Förnyelsekraften genom nya produkter, processer och affärskoncept måste vara hög. Det är en förutsättning för att produktiviteten ska öka. Därför behövs forsknings- och utvecklingsarbete både inom och utom företagen som bidrar till att Sörmlands näringsliv växer och förnyas.

▸ 55

MÅL 3 – STRATEGIER

Figure 4.6 Representations of knowledge in regional development policy. Reproduction of page 55 in the regional development strategy of Region Sörmland (24:55).

knowledge actually is depicted and graphically represented in most plans but also that the images used to display this have such a distinct commonality. In Figure 4.6 we have reproduced what this looks like in a Swedish regional development strategy.

The commonality that we speak of is two-fold. On the one hand, it is about the setting. The laboratory, where some more or less high tech equipment and lab coats combine into a specific representation of expertise and knowledge that is important for the region in its strive for competitiveness. On the other hand, it is the inclusion of 'new' subjects in this image. Perhaps this second aspect is particularly pronounced in the Nordic countries; however, it is still a strong emphasis on, for instance, women and/or immigrants taking part in this advanced form of knowledge. We argue that this form of representation fits well with the overall rationality of competitiveness. First of all what is represented is often a combination of two knowledge domains, namely biotechnology and variations of information technology. These are often understood to be particularly important areas of knowledge for regions that aim to steer ahead of the competition in the years to come. Second of all, it is also important that this is a form of knowledge that seems to be translated into innovations and therefore can be used to harvest financial gains. If we think of it, knowledge could of course have been represented through images and graphics in many different ways. Sticking with the domain of biology, we could, for instance, have been shown a biologist that is doing field work, looking for fish in a river or, indeed, also a biologist doing some deep reading or writing. However, it is not primarily these aspects of biology that are supposed to help lift the region into a new reach in terms of competitiveness. As for the inclusion of new subjects, we argue that this is also in line with the main rationalities we discussed in Chapter 3. To be able to get ahead in the competition the region cannot afford to keep large parts of its potential outside of the ranks. Indeed, they can be viewed as untapped potential. We do not contest that such an inclusion is most likely represented with good intentions. That being said, it also signals a more problematic underlying message that seems to be true for more or less everything that is being done in contemporary regional development. The inclusion of new subjects is premised on their ability to contribute in the competitiveness wars. Simply put, if someone or something is not, it does not seem to be important in regional development at this point. In other words a range of fundamental democratic aspects, such as equal rights and possibilities among citizens regardless of gender or ethnicity are only important as long as they help boost competitiveness. What if it turns out that democracy is not good for competitiveness? Which principle is to prevail?

The third point that we wish to make concerning the multimodal policy documents that are being produced in regional development is related to what we call *comic policy*. By this we mean to draw attention to how a distinct form of multimodal policy has started to emerge in the context of regional development that through comic strips, or indeed, full comic albums, short films, and games (traditional board games, puzzles as well as digital web games) aim to communicate the rationality of competitiveness. Sometimes, like in the example portrayed in Figure 4.7 this is explicitly directed to youth and school children; at other times, there seem to be a need to communicate policy through 'comic' and 'simple' narratives.

We will not spend a lot of time here to semiotically analyze the way that the European Commission uses comic books; however, we find it important

Figure 4.7 Comic policy. Reproduction of page 24 in the 'Partners' comic issued by the Directorate-General for Regional and Urban Policy of the EC (25:24).

to point out how hegemonic the rationality of competitiveness is. This is not a cheap or unprofessional production. In terms of artistic quality and layout these could be taken from any popular mainstream comic these days, and the artists that have been invited to draw the six different tales of the so called *Partners* comic issued by the EC are all accomplished within the comic scene. Together with the online tools, jigsaw puzzles, and posters, the *Partners* comic stands at the center for an initiative to educate and promote the core rationalities of regional development to children. By stating that this is an expression of the hegemonic character of the rationalities detailed in Chapter 3, we mean that this not at all seems controversial. Indeed, it is communicated as more or less non-political. The EU is an important figure in the comics and acts as a provider and supplier of funds to a range of mostly private entrepreneurs that are striving to realize their innovative ideas and products. However, there is very little politics here. No real conflicts of interests are portrayed, and concrete expressions of politics such as parliaments, debates, and politicians are more or less absent from all stories. Regional development, we learn, is seemingly carried out best without such distractions.

Finally, as part of this third point we wish to mention how comics and films are also being produced for audiences beyond school children and youth. In particular it seems as if the concept of smart specialization, for some reason, needs to be communicated in 'simple' ways. One of the most explicit such 'simple' illustrations is a film produced by the EC as part of its smart specialization initiative called *Smart Specialization – efficient and effective use of public investment in research*. Available on YouTube and other online sources, the film showcases cartoon characters in the Kingdom of Smart, where all is not well. For whatever reason, the king needs help to reinvigorate the people of his country that are apparently broke. His court of advisors suggests different things such as raising taxes, lowering taxes, closing borders, and other 'old' news. However, one advisor has an idea that she bravely enough presents to the king – smart specialization. It involves getting everybody, from dwarves and goblins to normal peasants, in the country to synchronize their efforts in research and entrepreneurship. The king is reluctant at first, but after some inspiring words from the young woman who dared to speak up on the concept he realizes its potential and so he adopts the smart specialization strategy. Like in the case with the *Partners* comic, this is professionally produced in terms of animation and filmmaking. There are a wide range of topics to discuss in relation to this film, however, for now we are satisfied with moving on to a summarizing discussion concerning the governmental technologies that we have been illustrating in this chapter and their relationship with traveling expertise.

Conclusion: technologies for and of expertise

In this chapter, we have detailed a selection of governmental technologies that work together with the rationalities presented in Chapter 3. In conjunction, they help produce the assemblage of traveling expertise that we are interested in. As such then, they help realize effects associated with this expertise and, in particular, we would like to conclude with one overarching such realization.

Consider, therefore, how the various forms of benchmarking, monitoring, and ranking drives the presence of expertise in regional development into a place within its core practices. The maintenance of such systems relies on a multitude of practices and expert bodies that forcefully carve out a space for themselves that is very rarely questioned. Indeed, this expertise is also for the most part external with respect to the formal governing bodies of regions throughout Europe and beyond. While one could make an argument that seems perfectly rational from the stand point of more classical Weberian takes on public administration that the bureaucrats working within it are well equipped to carry out these tasks by themselves, this is very seldom the message that echoes through the rationalities and technologies. Rather, the external monitoring is often considered to offer a particular form of objective and precise knowledge base for assessing the state of the competition as well as for predicting its future development. The way this is articulated through the governing rationalities is often particularly strong in terms of opposing an 'in-house' (as civil servants in our interviews chose to word it) responsibility for monitoring and evaluation. In this way, external technologies of expertise in the form of rankings, indices, and other benchmarking expressions lend the enacted rationalities a legitimation that they need to sustain themselves. Thus, as with the rationalities illustrated and portrayed in Chapter 3, the technologies that we have used as points of departure here can also be said to be *of*, as well as *for*, expertise.

This situation, where the technologies of expertise take form as core practices within regional development, makes even more room for a governing regime that is not based primarily in traditional structures found in politics. Indeed, the technologies further what we have eluded as forms of *depoliticization*. For now, however, we leave that discussion aside and return to it in the final chapter of the book. Before that, we would like to make a final note on what we may label the *surveillance* effect that arises from the technologies illustrated here. Notice how they are designed in ways that suggest a constant self-monitoring for the leadership of any region. The ways the technologies assemble expertise into visible and interactive representations of benchmarking allows, not only for others to view a particular region's position and result, but rather, it allows any given region to act upon how others view them. This realization is a powerful incentive for a form of self-governing with respect to the regions struggling to gain positions in the competition. Particularly so since the rationalities at work here tie together present positions in the quest for competitiveness with future abilities to attract resources and talents.

In the next chapter we turn to what we call the subjects of expertise, or in other words, how various actors shape and take shape in regional development as rationalities and technologies of traveling expertise link up, merge, and draw out the trajectories for governing.

5   Subjectivities

One of us got an email. An invitation to participate in discussions and activities that would help bring the region into new domains of competitiveness. The organizer of this event tried to reach 'creative people' who could contribute during two days and brainstorm on how to boost entrepreneurship and innovation. It would be sort of like TED-talks, yet not TED-talks, the invitation said. More loose. An opportunity for any of the invited creative people to take the stage when they felt they had something to say. It sounded strange, yet intriguing. On social network apps, it was possible to trace some of the other people who had been invited. Entrepreneurs, designers, other researchers, programmers, policy makers, and others of similar status. In this sense the event felt familiar.

They keep appearing. Regardless of setting. The faces change, yet feel so very familiar. Not only among the actual attendees, but also in the stories, images, and films that stand at the center of the events. In a context of immigration, we hear of and speak of untapped potential entrepreneurs. At that conference that promoted the outmost importance of gender equality in urban and regional development, we learned that competitiveness and growth would get such a boost if women were to be empowered to let loose their innovative capacity as programmers and leaders. And so the story goes.

Indeed, similar things have happened many times to the both of us. As a researcher, you qualify as a category of people that are highly sought for in regional development. So, it starts to add up. Panel discussions, seminars, deliberations, and conferences to which we are invited and made a part of. While we as researchers certainly are aware of how most contemporary policies emphasize this 'creative class' of people in conjunction with possibilities to produce growth, we also agree on the mixed feeling of experiencing these subjectivities. Not reading about them, experiencing them. They are hard to resist. And we actually don't think that we are anymore able to resist or escape the positioning we are ascribed than the others that gather at these occasions. When we step in there, and even before, when we get the invitation, the structure interpellates us, to use the famous concept of Althusser. It calls us out. Forces us to act within a given frame. So, who are we, the subjects of regional development? Who are we not? How does this matter?

Who is who in regional development?

In the warlike discourse of regional development that we have alluded to there is a dimension that we so far have not drawn on in terms of metaphors.

Now is probably the time to do so. Consider therefore how in the struggle for resources and development the global competition calls for specific roles in terms of its troops. What actions are not only desirable but also possible with consideration to the forces available for mobilization? How can the battle be coordinated in a way that gives the best odds for survival? Where is there a need for reinforcements? These are the issues we activate in this chapter.

In the tradition of governmentality studies, one of the main analytical interests is to understand *how* social actors are articulated in relation to political rationalities and governmental technologies. This *how* includes the assumptions behind both which specific actors that are included and excluded as relevant in the domain of governing that is analyzed and also how they are positioned in the grand narrative of regional development and related to each other. The subjectivities cannot just be viewed as an effect of a specific political rationality or governmental technology, but they also constitute and articulate the same. They are neither reducible to, nor possible to isolate from, each other. On the contrary, the analysis of subjectivities will contribute with a deeper understanding on how the rationalities and technologies are assembled and legitimized as a 'reason' or a reasonable way to understand and govern social reality (Dean, 2010; See Mansfield, 2000). Mitchel Dean (2010:43) explains the interest in subjectivities – or identity formations – from a governmentality perspective, in the following way:

> …[W]hat forms of person, self and identity are presupposed by different practices of government and what sorts of transformation do these practices seek? What statuses, capacities, attributes and orientations are assumed of those who exercise authority (from politicians and bureaucrats to professionals and therapists) and those who are to be governed (workers, consumers, pupils and social welfare recipients)? What forms of conduct are expected of them? What duties and rights do they have? How are these capacities and attributes to be fostered? How are these duties enforced and rights ensured? How are certain aspects of conduct problematized? How are they then to be reformed? How are certain individuals and populations made to identify with certain groups, to become virtuous and active citizens, and so on?

When using the terms actors, subjectivities, and identities in this way, it is important to denote that it does not refer to autonomous subjects with the intention to understand or map the intentions, convictions, and inner drivers of those subjects. Rather, it is an analysis that aims to capture action, but not the action of specific actors. Instead, the action that this form of analysis takes interest in is the act of 'subjectification' (Miller & Rose 2008:8) through articulation of meaning. We approach the material with the question of how actors, subjects, and identities are constructed and molded in relation to the grand narrative of regional development. As the terrain of regional development is understood as increasingly globalized and the rationalities of global competition and attractiveness become stronger, we turn our attention to how the identities of agents and actors are shaped by such overarching transformations in the policy field. The main reason for this analytical task is to be able to discuss who is included and who is excluded in the dominating ways of bringing meaning to the region and regional development. But also, who is constructed as important, wanted, and desired and who is a liability, a threat or simply irrelevant in the competitive region as parts and effects of how regional development is governed.

In the text, we talk both about *social actors* and *subjectivities*. By social actors we refer to when actors are explicitly mentioned and articulated in the empirical material and the way that they are explicitly produced with specific characteristics, roles or functions for regional development. When we use the term subjectivities as an analytical category we refer to the ways that these social actors are given meaning in relation to the political rationalities and governmental technologies of regional development. We use subjectivities to categorize and name what we see as central *types of identities* in the material. In this sense the term social actor is closer to the empirical material and subjectivity is a more abstract term to discuss the governmentality of regional development.

In the empirical illustrations of this chapter, we turn to texts and empirical material that in different ways articulate the meaning of social actors in relation to regional development and the role of expertise. This includes policy documents, assessment reports, and other documents within the field. As the chapter progresses, we will move closer to examining how the social actors that are directly connected to notions of expertise are articulated and how the rationalities of global competiveness are central for these specific articulations. For the illustrations of this chapter we have focused on the case of Sweden. We focus mainly on one empirical case to give an image of how the social actors are made meaningful through how they are related to each other in a specific context. However, even though there will be some particular traits of the Swedish case (such as the priority of gender equality in regional development policy) our intention is still to illustrate a broad understanding of the social actors of regional development in Europe and beyond. Sweden is, in this case, not a deviant case. In the following section, we move the analysis forward in three steps: The first step is a more general analysis how the grand narrative of regional development constructs a frame to articulate the meaning and position of social actors in a way that relates to the globalized understanding of regional competitiveness. In the second step, we go to examine in greater detail a selection of social actors to illustrate the specific form that they are given against this backdrop. In the third step, we summarize in a concluding way how the social actors can be seen as categorized in three different kinds of subjectivities and discuss the ways they are related to the grand narrative of regional development.

Central social actors for regional development

In a first step, we would like to illustrate how the overarching rationalities of global competitiveness activates and articulates a specific understanding of social actors. In this quote the Swedish Globalization Council express how global competition is changing the rules of development in a way that puts some regions in the foreground of being successful in this struggle for resources.

> Globalization and especially the extensive economic integration in Europe make it less and less important for companies to locate their activities to a certain market or a certain country. Instead, it is becoming even more valuable to place activities in an attractive cluster. The competition between European countries for attractive companies will therefore turn more and more into a competition between major European urban centers. This is an opportunity for Sweden, a country which is otherwise disadvantaged by a small market. The conclusion of this report is that it is crucial for Sweden's future growth potential that the major metropolitan regions can continue developing as successful service-industrial clusters and that Sweden succeeds in attracting and retaining a critical mass if human capital and individuals with top-level competence. This means several challenges in the domain of financial politics.
>
> (26:52)

The quote illustrates that the game changing rules of global competition have an impact on how it makes sense to think about strategic policy development for regions. The market of globally mobile capital is viewed as unreachable for regulations. However, it is possible to anticipate how capital moves and adapt policies accordingly. A number of actors or subjectivities are mentioned in the quote, each with a specific role to play in the rationality of global competition. The first actor, the countries, and in this quote specifically Sweden, play the role of competitors in this global terrain of capital and resources. Even though they are not understood as the main interest for mobile capital, they are articulated as the contenders, struggling for the scarce resources of attractive companies to settle down within their territory. For Sweden, this shift is described as a benefit, a condition that enables Sweden to be successful in securing resources for development.

The second actor that is drawn in to the foreground of the dynamics of global competitiveness is the metropolitan urban regions. These regions are articulated as the key actors to actually be successful in the global struggle for resources. It is the metropolitan regions that can adapt according to the demands that make a place attractive for companies to settle down. The quote articulates how such regions must be prioritized and strategically developed to be globally attractive through regional development policy initiatives.

The third actor that is structured against the backdrop of global competition is the individuals with top-level competences. These actors are articulated both as crucial for making the metropolitan regions attractive for companies and also as a form of capital or a resource that needs to be attracted to the region. The challenge for regional development policy seems to be to attract the right individuals to regions in order to be attractive for companies to settle down in the region.

The fourth actor is the companies. The companies are understood as the resources that can develop the region and the country. The companies are, in this quote, the prize that the countries and the regions are competing for. The winner is the region that can attract the globally mobile companies to settle down, and the winning development strategy is to strategically transform the region into a place that would be attractive for the companies.

If we take a step back and think about how this discursive backdrop of global competition configures specific relationships between these actors, we can see that embedded in these articulations are specific power relations and discursive practices of inclusion/exclusion. For instance, the relationship between the country, or the central state, and the region is described in a way that makes the state more incapable and the region capable when it comes to driving policies for regional development. The metropolitan urban regions must be understood in relation to their not-mentioned outside; the non-urban regions that do not seem to play a key role in regional development. The individuals with top-level competences play a key role in contrast with individuals that do not hold top level competences. And the companies' preferences seem to set the criteria for what an attractive region is, preferences for the regional policy makers to try to interpret, anticipate, and adapt their policies accordingly.

We can also see that there are some pretty advanced dynamics articulated in the quote, which explain how these actors interact, or should interact, in order to be successful in regional development endeavors. One particularly complex dynamic is the relationship between the region, the individuals with top-level competence, and the companies. The regions are looking for companies to settle; the way to achieve that is to be attractive to the companies. And the companies need a critical mass of individuals with top-level competences. In order to be attractive for companies, the regions must make themselves attractive for individuals with top level competences. This casual chain of development correlates strongly with the theory of the creative class, as put forward by Richard Florida where he explicitly describes who the desired individuals are and why they are so crucial for regional growth:

> The Super-Creative Core of this new class includes scientists and engineers, university professors, poets and novelists, artists, entertainers, actors, designers and architects, as well as the thought leadership of modern society: nonfiction writers, editors, cultural figures, think-tank researchers, analysts and other opinion-makers... Beyond this group the Creative

Class also includes "creative professionals" who work in a wide range of knowledge intensive industries such as high-tech sectors, financial services, the legal and health care professions, and business management.

(Florida, 2002:69)

Florida's assumption is that the concentration of creative class in a city or a region will determine the attractiveness for companies to settle in the region. The reason for this is that the creative class makes the necessary added value for being innovative, and innovation is truly viewed as the key for growth and successful enterprise. In regional policies, there are mainly two ways to work with the concentration of individuals with top-level competence. One is to work with and cultivate the population already living in the region, and the other is to attract desired people from outside the region. In OECD's Territorial review of the region Skåne in Sweden the following is expressed:

Opportunities to deepen the region's labor markets are twofold. In the first place, Skåne should work to capitalize on its strong innovative environment, expanding its entrepreneurial base. Substantial regional investment in the promotion of entrepreneurialism has rendered Skåne one of the most dynamic Swedish regions in terms of the proportions of newly created enterprises in total enterprises, but the region has the smallest proportion of firms created by those holding no more than compulsory education. Policies to promote innovation among a more extensive base of potential entrepreneurs, though training and enhanced access to capital for migrants, women and youth, would help to deepen regional labor markets, providing more employment opportunities for the region's expanding population. A second opportunity to deepen local labor markets lies in the region's ability to attract skilled international workers, providing an attractive environment to encourage them, and their families, to locate in the region.

(27:19)

This quote shows explicitly how the notion of top-level competences is constructed in relation to specific groups. The most striking example in the quote is perhaps the differentiation between skilled international workers who are desired for their role to contribute to regional development and immigrants who need to be trained to go from a 'base of potential entrepreneurs' to actual contributors, just as youth and women.

The point of these illustrations is to show how the rationalities of regional competition and attractiveness are also having direct effects for how different identities are produced as relevant, irrelevant, assets, liabilities, desired, and undesired. The rationality functions as a discursive backdrop to make it sensible to differ between immigrants and skilled international workers, top-level competences, women, and internal and external entrepreneurs. In the following sections of this chapter we will look closer on how these identities are constructed as social actors and how they are positioned in the grand narrative of regional development. We will turn our attention to five different actors that are given importance in regional development policy throughout our empirical material. In other words, we will illustrate in a more detailed way how they are given specific positions in, and act as vehicles for, the rationalities that structure the field of regional development. The actors are *the region, the corporation, the women, the immigrants, and the experts.*

The region

We have already touched upon the effects of how the role of regions have changed with the increasing understanding of regions as operating in a global terrain and given more autonomy to do so, in line with the development of new regionalism reforms. However, in order to understand regions as actors in a more detailed way, we want to illustrate how these understandings are described and motivated in policy texts. We want to emphasize three aspects of how the region is constructed in the material. First, how the region is understood as *important*, second how the region is understood as *re-active*, and finally how the region is understood as *differentiated*.

The importance of the region is broadly made sensible in articulations that position the region in a global terrain; explanations of how the processes of globalization are relevant for understating what regions have become or what role they are supposed to play in this transforming environment. In the final report of the Swedish Committee on Public Responsibility the following is expressed:

> Economic globalization has made companies less dependent on national borders and governments, at the same time as increasing competition and specialization create higher demands on competence provision, logistics and an attractive living environment to attract coworkers. Many of these needs are filled most effectively on a geographical scale in between local and national levels, and therefore require regional areas of contact for the public sector and society at large.
>
> (28:195)

The quote illustrates the main argument for the increasing importance of regions as a function of economic globalization. Although the quote can be viewed as a rather passive articulation of regions, the importance of regions to operate in a global environment is not seen as passive. On the contrary, it is one of the main arguments why regions must be equipped with a stronger autonomy from the state to be able to be effective in managing this new responsibility, as exemplified below by the Swedish Association of Local Authorities and Regions:

> At a time when regions compete in the arena of attracting people and businesses, the need increases for an internationally competitive institution with an explicit growth commission. Sweden needs stronger regions capable of operating across borders.
>
> (29:3)

In short, the region as an actor operating on a global arena is understood as the answer to how to survive and be successful in these new globalized conditions for development. And the strategic significance of equipping regions with what they need to operate under these new conditions is clearly stressed. It is, however, important to note that this autonomy from the state, this mandate to operate, is not articulated as a freedom to govern themselves, perusing whatever visions or objectives they would formulate as development. It is a mandate to adapt to already formulated conditions and constructions that are viewed as given or natural. It is the system of globalized capitalism that conducts the terms and the role of more autonomous regions is to adapt as successfully as possible to these terms. This form of 'autonomy' should therefore not be confused as just self-governing for the region. The political objectives and trajectories are not to be determined through democratic deliberation in the way that it is articulated in the material. This form of empowerment, or increasing mandate for regions to take action, must be understood as a mandate or a responsibility to be *re-active* to the processes and events that are determined from outside the region. In this sense, the empowerment and increasing autonomy for region – in perhaps a paradoxical way – contributes to a depoliticization of regional politics and development policy. It is a freedom to surrender to the conditions of globalized capitalism in the most effective way.

The third aspect of how the region is articulated as a social actor is about *differentiation*. With differentiation, we want to emphasize how importance, progress, success, and development are understood both within and between regions. Within regions, perhaps the clearest example of differentiation related to regional development is the divide between the urban and the rural parts of a region. The urban – or metropolitan – centers are articulated as nodes of growth and innovation, as the key areas to develop and prioritize in order to be successful in the global struggle for resources. The rural areas are mainly articulated as passive, in need to be better connected (through technology or increased mobility) to the urban centers to be able to play any significant role for regional development. In the same manner, there is a *differentiation* on how regions are understood to be related to each other. As in the case with the relationship between rural and urban areas, regions and cities are also articulated as related in a network to other regions and cities and those relationships become crucial for developing the region. Smaller regions and cities that are deemed too small to compete on a global market are articulated with a need to be connected to larger regions and cities to be successful. The global metropolitan cities are understood as having a central role for the patterns of the network of regions and cities:

> Globally connected cities will continue to attract human capital and cluster higher added value activities. Europe, while hosting a few large metropolis, above 10 million people, has a balanced distribution of small and medium-sized cities all over the territory. Considering the challenges that global cities may have in terms of overconcentration, which could

hamper sustainable growth, the polycentric structure of the European territory and the already large fixed social capital investments allocated in many cities, have the potential to facilitate a more balanced growth. European small and medium sized cities will have to increase their European and global connectivity without losing their social inclusiveness and cultural heritage.

(30:21)

The network of differentiation fosters logics that affect how specific regions and cities develop and apply policy strategies for regional development. There is a constant drive to be connected to a bigger or more successful region, and the logic also induces an acceptance for regional differences, which sometimes leaves substantial challenges for smaller regions. As articulated here in a regional development strategy document adopted by the Örebro region in Sweden:

> The location of Örebro 200 kilometers from Stockholm and even further from Gothenburg and Oslo makes it unlikely that we will turn into an integrated, functional part of either of these regions. The functional region of Stockholm will probably comprise most of the counties of Västmanland, Sörmland, and Uppland but only in certain specific cases include parts of the county of Örebro. At the same time, our region is probably too small for us to be able to create solid growth on our own. We are a region with a city which is slightly smaller than the definition of a big city. We cannot, unlike Stockholm, Malmö, Gotherburg – and possibly in the long run, Norrköping-Linköping – expect the size of the region in itself to guarantee sustainable growth and welfare.

(31:14)

To summarize, the region is articulated as a social actor of central importance for strategically working for development and growth, is seen as mostly reactive to the conditions of global competition for resources, and the regions are understood as internally and externally attached to a network of differentiation.

The corporation

The corporations as social actors within the rationalities of regional development are placed at the very core of global competition and function as the main drivers for development and prosperity in any given region. The corporations are represented in the material with a double functional role for regional development: as the object of competition – the resource that regions are trying to attract – and also as an important feature of regional competitiveness. This is because the right kind of corporations are understood to be increasing the regions' attractiveness for other resources (other corporations, well educated people, etc.).

The corporation as a social actor is represented as extremely mobile and hyper rational when it comes to choosing its location to settle down. That being said, they are also represented to exhibit a quite elusive and even volatile behavior that is hard to control. This, in combination with the fundamental role they are assumed to play for development makes the strategic importance of offering an environment that is highly corporation-friendly. Thus, to be able to show some form of added value for corporations if they would be located in the region is a fundamental part of any policy that aims for global competitiveness. In the Swedish government's national strategy for regional growth and attraction such strategic added values are articulated in the following way:

> A policy for promoting entrepreneurship and growing businesses include framework conditions, incentives, and targeted measures. Sweden needs a business climate where many people, regardless of age, gender and background, can identify opportunities and be willing to take risks, but also have access to the resources and support systems that they may need at critical stages of development. For instance, the ability to facilitate things for companies, to attract, keep, and develop skills, create access to capital, and take advantage of international contacts, is also greatly significant for the regional development potential. The public sector should contribute to these functions as parts of its areas of responsibility.
>
> (02:13)

As the quote illustrates, the responsibility to create and maintain a corporation-friendly environment rests on the shoulders of public policy makers, in this case the regional development agencies. The details and nuances of how aspects of corporate mobility is represented within the field of regional development also show that even if a corporation choses to relocate or start a branch in a region it does not mean that the competition is over. Rather, the competition is a permanent state. Therefore, it is crucial to maintain relevance and value addition even after such a settlement or startup. This dimension of corporation mobility is described in the following way by a Swedish think-tank called Globalization Forum:

> A recent trend is that multinational companies to a greater extent also locate R&D in different countries. R&D has often been characterized as more place-specific than production, in the sense that R&D activities have normally been localized to the home countries of the companies and close to the head office (Patel and Pavit 1991). The globalization of the R&D activities of multinational companies is a recent phenomenon that has developed at a slower pace than the globalization of production (Carlsson 2006). Today, the multinational companies (including the Swedish ones) run extensive R&D operations around the world.

A survey made by Tillväxtanalys regarding multinational companies in Sweden also show that a majority of companies, almost two thirds, think that the location of the head office is not particularly important for the localization of other strategic operations such as R&D.

(32)

The quote illustrates a dimension of global mobility for the corporations, that goes beyond strictly the physical localization. From a regional development perspective, this means that the challenge of global competition is not only about attracting corporations but also to remain attractive for the desired parts of 'global value chains' and the innovative branches within already settled corporations. Strategically working for a good business climate to ensure competitiveness for corporations is thus both a long-term and a short-term endeavor for regional policy makers. Also, the global mobility of corporation settlements as well as investments must constantly be taken into consideration.

Besides the large scale, multinational, global perspective of competitiveness, the way that corporations are represented as actors in the material are also articulated within the region. In policy strategies and other documents of the data we draw on, business climate and corporations are represented so that it allows two distinct interpretations, or ways of making sense, of the existing businesses within the region. The first way is about making sure that new corporations can be easily started and that there are sufficient support structures to lower the thresholds for new business ideas to be transformed in to up-and-running corporations. The second way is to strategically cooperate within the region to coordinate around strategic business branches (through agglomeration, cluster formation or SMART specialization) to add value for the region as a global player within a more specific niche of business.

This two-folded perspective of the corporation as a social actor in the field of regional development can be understood as a way of managing the complex relations between the regional and the global, and between competition and cooperation. The characteristics of the behavior of corporations outside the region, marked by the conditions of globalized capitalism such as elusive and highly mobile capital and resources, spur the need for corporations within the region to cooperate and unite in order to be more successful at the frontline of the global struggles. The cooperation between corporations within the region can also be understood in the light of how the mechanisms of regional growth are articulated in the material. Often, innovation and knowledge are described as the drivers for regional development, and within the regions the smaller corporations must work together in order to foster an innovative *milieu* that the multi-national corporations have the economic muscle to achieve within their corporative structures. In these cooperations, businesses should not only coordinate with each other, they should also interact with the public sector and academia in order to achieve such an innovative environment. The way this reasoning about the need for cooperation is expressed in our material can be illustrated by the quote below from a regional development plan:

> In an ever more competitive situation, the ability to change continually is required for a company to survive. The businesses in southern Småland cannot respond to increasing global competition with lower salaries and simple production, but only through development and innovation. A good climate for innovation creates conditions for knowledge and entrepreneurship to lead up to new products and services, or new modes of production. Innovations are dependent on a highly functional interplay between those agents who influence the way in which knowledge is created and used in the business sector, in politics, and in research. Apart from the role of physical capital, financial capital, and human capital, the dimension of social capital has become more and more important – a social capital which consists partly of the access of people and businesses to social networks, and partly of the level of trust between these agents. The focus is moved from effective production to the ability to cooperate and the need for a creative and tolerant environment.
>
> (07:7)

Thus, this dual function of corporations in the dynamics of competitiveness and regional development is constructed in connection to the region. Therefore, a main objective for policy makers is to adjust and fine-tune the relationship between the internal corporations through cooperation, coordination, specialization, and cross-sectorial collaborations and aligning those internal corporations with what makes that specific environment attractive for actors on the global market. The importance of such strategic operations, as well as the connection between the conditions within the region and in the global terrain, can be exemplified by the national innovation strategy issued by the Swedish government:

> It is highly desirable that the development of regional innovation environments in Sweden is coupled with a strategic approach to international development. A special potential for sustainable growth and innovation in the regional economy resides in the connection between different industries and fields of knowledge. The creation of meeting places, for instance in the form of clusters or networks, is therefore valuable innovative edge and regional growth. Cooperation in these innovative environments can promote innovation and competitive power, and create conditions for them to become attractive nodes in global knowledge and innovation networks and platforms for cooperation on the regional, national, and international level. A development of the tourism industry and the cultural and creative sectors can also contribute to more attractive innovation environments. These industries are characterized by

strong growth internationally, and Sweden has the potential to increase export and value creation in these areas.

(33:48)

To summarize, corporations as social actors are represented in the material in two different but strategically interlinked ways. First, as the large-scale, resourceful, multinational actors whose interests and needs dominate the conditions of regional development. They are the prize of the global competition and in order to win, the region must attract their attention through tailor cut strategies. Second, the small scale internal businesses that are important for regional growth since they help put in place and facilitate an innovative, creative environment that could serve as an added value for future investments.

The women

The way women are represented as social actors in the material is related to the policy goal of regional gender equality, which is present throughout the material. From the European Union notions on inclusive growth, gender mainstreaming, and gender equality related to the EU2020 program, through national strategies and programs down to the specific regional policies women emerge as prominent social actors in regional development. That being said, the way they are being represented is primarily as disenfranchised, in need of empowerment and help. While the representations obviously vary with nuances and details, we argue that women are produced in two main ways here. The first specific representation of women in the material is in relationship to gender equality as a policy goal. The second, related, representation of women as social actors in regional development emphasizes how women are potential assets for innovation and entrepreneurship in the region. As this happens, women are ascribed a specific meaning in relation to how they can contribute to innovation and regional competitiveness.

If we start with the first representation related to gender equality, the basic notion is that men and women have different opportunities in life and that this must be addressed. However, this is rarely represented as a power relation between men and women. In fact, throughout the material the causes of these differences and inequalities are not really addressed at all. More commonly, the different conditions for men and women are described as an unfortunate state that everybody has to gain from changing. Below is an example of a quote that actually explicitly describes gender equality as related to power, but never explains the dynamics of those power relations. The quote comes from a regional development plan in Sweden:

Equality contributes to regional development through granting everyone the same opportunity to contribute to social development. Studies have shown that women as a group have less power and influence than men in relation to social development today. Among other things, men are more prevalent in leading positions in the business sector while women earn less doing the same jobs and assume more responsibility for the domestic sphere. Västerbotten starts out from the Swedish objective for equality politics, the idea that women and men should occupy the same position of power in terms of being able to shape both society and their own lives.

(34:6)

In this quote, men and women as groups with different access to power are clearly described in a way that is not typical for the material. It is however described in a general way and the description does not explain the causes of this state of inequality, which actually is typical for the material. The lack of gender equality seems to be understood as an unfortunate flaw in the system that simply needs correction. For some irrational reason women seem to be held back. Now, this lacking analysis or articulation of why women are held back makes us have to turn to the solutions to find representations of what the causes of the problem might be. In the following quote, the OECD articulates how gender equality should be promoted through regional development policies:

Enhancing women's entrepreneurship benefits from renewed international impetus, including the ongoing OECD Gender Initiative (Box 316). More specifically, experience in some OECD countries has suggested that monitoring programs from women to women have higher potential to foster female entrepreneurship effectively. Such programs aim to offer a useful bridge towards role models that are available to transfer successful experiences to potential entrepreneurs and to increase the latter's self-confidence. At the European level, the European Network of Mentors for Women Entrepreneurs was inaugurated in Warsaw, Poland in November 2011. This network complements the actions that started with the creation of the European Network of Female Entrepreneurship Ambassadors (ENFEA) in 2009. It will provide advice and support to women entrepreneurs on the start-up, running and growth of their enterprises in their early phase of their life (from the second to their fourth year of existence of a new women-run and owned enterprise). The Women Entrepreneurship Portal also offers a list of national and international organizations that provide advice, support, information and contact regarding existing support measures for female entrepreneurs. In Sweden, ALMI Företagspartner AB will receive SEK 30 million per year to strengthen women entrepreneurship through a variety of mentoring programs, training and funding instruments. Special efforts will be made to reach women in green industries, the service sector, creative and cultural industries, health and social care, and education.

(27:214)

The quote illustrates a hands-on strategy to work for gender equality through support, advice, mentorship, and networks for women entrepreneurs. It does not explicitly point out why we are in a situation where women are disenfranchised to begin with; however, it is clear that the solution lies in handling a series of lacks or flaws that can be found in women entrepreneurs today; one being the lack of self-confidence. The path to equality seems, in this representation, to be about educating and improving the women's entrepreneurial skills to navigate out of their unfortunate position. In this sense the root of the gender equality problem, as far as it is described, seems to be the women themselves, the lack of power and influence seems to be about their lacking skills and self-confidence compared to others (men).

In the second kind of representation in the material the role of women as social actors is related to their potential to contribute to innovation and growth. This representation is less driven by equality as a matter of justice or power and more by the notion of women as an untapped source of regional growth, as expressed here in a regional development plan from Dalarna region, Sweden:

> Women's and men's equal contributions to and influence over innovation work and the job market is becoming an ever more critical growth factor. A greater degree of equality supports the successful matching of skills for business needs, improves the conditions for entrepreneurship and innovative edge in Dalarna and also contributes to make Dalarna more attractive. In Dalarna, as in other neighboring regions, the business sector and the job market are greatly segregated in terms of gender. Growth could be strengthened in Dalarna if such patterns where abandoned.
>
> (35:5)

The quote illustrates an important notion of the legitimacy for working towards gender equality that is present throughout the material: gender equality has a functional advantage in promoting regional growth. In this representation of women in regional development, empowerment is not about justice or equality for equality's own sake. This way of legitimizing gender equality work raises questions about what happens with policy ideas and proposals that do not increase and even might be counterproductive for regional growth. And one has to ask the question 'what happens to gender equality as a policy goal if it no longer is viewed as a way to liberate a potential source of growth?'

These representations seem to motivate the need for gender equality from two different angles. The first from a perspective, or a rationale, of justice – drawing from the injustice of women having a more disenfranchised position in society than men, and the second one from a functional perspective, where gender equality is viewed as a mean to the end or regional innovation and growth. In the Swedish government's action plan for regional growth the relationship between these two bases of legitimacy for gender equality work is described in the following way:

> The other connection involves the link between equality and democracy and the fact that greater equality contributes to a stronger democracy, which in turn supports the creation of conditions for increased growth. A society which does not exclude people from access to capital, networks, institutions, and so on, contributes to greater diversity, more trust, and a feeling of being a part of the community. Growing trust and diversity in social contacts also increase the chances for cooperation among businesses and public organizations which in turn supports the potential for innovation in society as a whole. An important aspect of democracy is to boost women's and men's ability to make their own choices as well as realize and commercialize their ideas.
>
> (36:3)

The quote illustrates not only the two representations of why gender equality is a legitimate policy goal to strive for – justice and functionality – but also merges the representations as intrinsic to democracy. Both the right to make choices over your own life and the right to commercialize your ideas. And most notably democracy seems to be viewed as legitimate for its capacity to facilitate economic growth.

In sum, the way that women are represented as social actors in the material follows two main trajectories, both related to the policy goal of gender equality: one that emphasizes power and justice and the other that emphasizes women as an untapped potential for growth. Both representations avoid explaining the reason for inequality; however, they both find the solution for lacking gender equality in helping women developing their skills, knowledge, entrepreneurship, and self-confidence to reach the same potential as men.

The immigrants

The representation of immigrants as social actors in the material is in many ways based on similar articulations for women. In other words, they are represented as a disenfranchised group in need of empowerment structures to fulfill all of its potential. There is, however, in contrast to women a more diversified understanding of different subcategories of immigrants that play different parts in the dynamics of regional development. First, we will illustrate how immigrants are understood as an untapped resource in a more general understanding before we go deeper into the different subcategories.

Immigrants are represented as a possible asset, or of importance for regional development in at least three ways in the material. First, immigrants are viewed as an asset to battle structural challenges of population composition in regions. This is particularly true for regions that experience problems with a decreasing and aging population due to the mobility of younger people that tend to be drawn to bigger urban centers. Immigrants can in this way help to counter the effects of such structural development if they are distributed accordingly. Secondly, immigrants are represented as an important value in relation to how a creative, attractive region or city is understood. Tolerance and multi-culturalism are expressed as values and features of a modern, open, and attractive society. Immigrants play an important role for creating the modern, urban vibe that is articulated as attractive for regions and cities in the global competition for investments and people. Thirdly, a specific sub-set of immigrants are represented as a group of highly skilled entrepreneurs, investors, business leaders, researchers, engineers, and students that have a special role to play for innovation and growth in the regional development.

In general, the representation of immigrants in our material is positive and welcoming. In the quote below from a regional development plan in a Swedish region the two first aspects of this representation that we mentioned above are readily visible:

> One way to respond to the great demographic challenges of the county is to focus on increased in-migration and labor migration as well as introduction activities for newly arrived inhabitants. The diversity brought to our region by people from other countries is valuable for competence and labor provisions but also for the development of our culture. We will therefore create good conditions for newly arrived inhabitants, regardless of background, to stay in our region, establish themselves on the job market, and take part actively in the development of the community. We can do this for instance by offering high quality schools, good housing, a creative work life and active participation in club activities.
>
> (37:30)

However, this welcoming representation of immigrants and viewing immigration as an asset for the region must also be understood in a more differentiated way. Indeed, in the governing rationalities of regional development there is a form of stratification of immigrants where one group, the highly skilled ones, are represented as the gems for which nations and regions compete. If successful in this particular competition, regions will be able to harvest talent and skills that are otherwise hard to come by. In the quote below this differentiation is illustrated by the final report for the ESPON project TIGER:

> In the context of globalized human flows, one of the major issues for Europe is to attract highly qualified labor (WP11 and 13). This specific migration plays a predominant role in many respects. Demographic trends might result in shortage of qualified labor, at least in some professions. Also, highly skilled labor is of utmost importance in knowledge transfer,

notably within major transnational firm's networks. [...] This might reflect the fact that migration to Europe in particular is more often of lower
skilled nature and that qualifications are not easily transferred. Overall,
Europe still lags behind the US in terms of high-skilled immigration,
but performs better than Japan. However, the trend of high-skilled migration to Europe is positive since Europe had displayed stronger growth
than the US in both absolute and per capita terms.

(38:16)

This division between high- and low-skilled immigrants shows that the welcoming attitude to immigration is more complex. Some groups of immigrants bring knowledge and skills that are wanted and needed and others
bring qualifications that are harder to make use of and their role for regional
development has to be thought about differently. It is the low-skilled immigrants that are in need of empowering structures in order to find their productive role in the region. In many cases this role is described as contributing
to the kind of environment that would attract the high-skilled immigrants.
That is, as service sector workers but also as features in a multi-cultural urban environment that would appeal to the high skilled immigrants. The following quote comes from OECD's territorial review of the Skåne region in
Sweden:

Governance partnerships between municipalities and local firms could
help tap into the existing and potential qualifications of the migrant labor force. An interesting example of a bottom-up partnership between
local government and local industry can be found in Malmö. During the
spring of 2011, many hotels in Malmö asked the city government for help
in finding asylum seekers who could work in the hotel industry in order
to better address the need of increasing numbers of international guests.
In the summer of 2011, the City of Malmö started offering a program of
adult education combined with Swedish language education and work-
place training for asylum seekers, with the promise that if participants
achieved a set of given standards they would then secure a job in a hotel.
Only 30 spots where available but the initiative attracted as many as 300
participants, and 23 out of the 30 candidates found jobs within 2 months.
Similar projects could be encouraged in the future, including other sectors, such as healthcare, which need professionals able to communicate
in foreign languages. The multi-national group of IKEA is currently
building a new conference center and a hotel in Malmö that will host
training programs for their employees from all over the world. Combined with targeted training mechanisms, this could be used as a pivotal
opportunity to harness the diversity of languages and other professional
skills available within the region's migrant labor force and bolster Skåne's
international brand.

(27:187)

The class dimension of how immigrants are both divided and thought to play different roles in the region is obvious. The low-skilled immigrants can find their role in the hotels, conference centers, health care, and other service sectors to make the region an attractive multi-cultural place for those immigrants that directly contribute to innovation and growth through their education and creative skills.

In summary, the immigrants as social actors are described as an asset in the material. Immigrants contribute to the region as labor force, through bringing a wanted multiculturalism to the region that is seen as an attractive aspect of being an attractive region in a globalized economy. Immigrants also bring competences into the region, which in different ways can contribute to growth and development. There is, however, a clear division in different kinds of immigrants – one low-skilled group in need of empowerment structures and pathways into the service sector to be able to play a role for growth and development and one high-skilled group that bring much needed talent in to the region, ready to contribute to innovation and the regional knowledge economy.

The experts

In this section, we turn to a category of social actors we call the experts. In this category, we find the subjects whose knowledge and expertise are articulated as crucial in the endeavors of being successful in regional development in this new era of globalized conditions. We have roughly divided this category into three kinds of experts that all play different but important roles for the region. First, there is the highly skilled internationally mobile expertise in specific fields that are identified as crucial to innovation and growth, the super creative core; the students, the researchers, and the business leaders, etc. Second, there are the future experts that can be cultivated within the region; in other words, those that do not have to be attracted on an international market of talent and knowledge. That is the researchers and the students of higher education within the region. Third, there are the policy experts that play different roles in producing knowledge needed to navigate in the global conditions of regional development; input for strategic policy design, evaluation, assessments, and 'evidence based' knowledge needed to develop policies and strategies for regional development and growth. This could be actors such as OECD, NORDREGIO, and ESPON.

The actors in this category have in common the knowledge and expertise, which are viewed as a crucial asset to be successful, but we want to roughly sort them in our analysis based on two distinct ways in which they function as assets: *experts as producers* and *experts as evaluators*. Now, there is no distinct line that separates the actors in these subcategories. One organization or expert can play both parts. However, in our material the need and value of expertise is distinctly articulated along these two functions and, therefore, want to examine them more closely and also show how they fit into the regional development narrative.

The first representation, *experts as producers* refers to those individuals with knowledge and expertise that are seen as highly mobile and prepared to relocate to a region or city that would offer them the best possibility to meet their preferences. This high mobility is seen as a constant state, which means that expertise in this sense is viewed as a rather volatile asset, continuously prepared to relocate. Indeed, in the common representations throughout our material, the highly skilled, well educated people with the much-needed productive knowledge and expertise for innovation and growth are represented as hyper-rational and constantly evaluating whether it is time to relocate the next region. Thus, much like in the case with the corporations, from a regional development perspective, the need to offer a living environment for the experts as producers is a crucial task in order to be successful:

> Sustainable growth in Sweden is not only dependent on the conditions for the business sector. It is also dependent on the environments where people live and work. Access to education, infrastructure, job markets, service, IT, culture, and housing is an important prerequisite for an attractive environment where people and companies can grow and work. Attractiveness is therefore a key requirement for sustainable growth and as such an obvious starting point for local and regional growth efforts. The ability to offer good living and housing environments is essential when creating regions that can attract, keep, and develop not only skills, but also businesses and capital.
>
> (MIEC, 2014a:2)

The need to consider the high mobility of this group is stressed by the Nordic council in their report *Global pressures Nordic solutions*, where the importance of attracting and keeping expertise in this sense is understood as a central key for the Nordic counties to become and stay globally competitive:

> Highly skilled employees and word-class research is the bedrock of Nordic competitiveness and the key reason for the high level of R&D intensity in the region. In both areas, the region is in danger of falling behind market needs, not the least because of a lack of a global perspective and Nordic integration. If there is one critical issue that the Nordics need to get right, it is this one.
>
> (04:7)

So, the experts as producers are represented as both crucial for regional development and as highly mobile. Thus, to underline this again, the regional policy makers' task is to transform the region in to an environment that meets the preferences of this group in order for them to want to relocate and also stay located in the region. This means that being able to foresee the preferences of this specific group and adapt accordingly is a central key to generating successful development policies for the region. This quote from a regional development plan in Jönköping, Sweden, gives a good illustration of how these preferences are imagined:

> A global living environment makes a city or town seem larger than it really is. A global living environment means that rural areas are connected to the world through good communications and increased digitalization, which results in a living, attractive, and socially functional countryside. A global living environment is a place where the outside world is an integrated part of the local community. It is characterized by curiosity about other cultures and it is creative and dynamic with an open and tolerant social climate which contributes to diversity. It is essential for a growing region both to keep and attract new inhabitants. People choose those towns and regions that offer the best balance of an interesting job market, dynamic living environments, attractive housing, community services, and a good environment for children and young people to grow up in.
>
> (40:28)

Urban centers connected to rural areas and the surrounding world, access to services, good housing, and a creative job market with a tolerant and multicultural attitude seem to be the core of how the preferences of the globally mobile *experts as producers* are represented in the material we mobilize here. In short, these features, which are often a mixture of place-specific amenities and global urban flows, need to be fostered and maintained if a region wants the expert producers to relocate and settle down in one of their cities.

When we turn to experts as evaluators, their role as experts functions quite differently. The productive expertise is understood as skills needed to facilitate growth through innovation and creativity – an ingredient articulated as crucial for the region to be globally competitive. The *evaluating expertise* is about knowing how to navigate and act strategically in the threatening global terrain of highly mobile capital and resources. In other words, the experts as evaluators will supply regional policy makers with the knowledge needed to develop appropriate policies in this global environment. The knowledge is seen as neutral, evidence based, and unbiased, which is central for legitimizing that policy makers are making the right strategic decision objectively for the region. The quote below illustrates the notion of such knowledge and hence the role of *experts as evaluators:*

> A key element in managing the territorial impact of policies is the availability of a sound "evidence base" of key EU territorial structures and processes, trends and methodologies. The need for territorial analyses and impact assessments was identified during the discussion on territorial cohesion and its policy implications which was launched by the European Commission after it had adopted its Green Paper on "Territorial Cohesion" in 2008. The key challenge is to produce targeted analyses for use at key moments in the whole EU policy process.

ESPON plays a crucial role in the development of a sound analytical base, and also in the development and use of methodologies for ex-ante territorial impact assessments of European Commission proposals. The first results of these researchers are already available from projects like TIPTAP or EDORA, for example. If the political will is there, these results could be used as a framework for a formal integrated impact assessment procedure. [...] The utilization and capitalization of ESPON results could also be developed at national and regional level. The whole ESPON program should be adapted to the needs of the period after 2013, in agreement of the European Commission, to better serve European policy making related to territorial development and cohesion.

(10:86)

The main point of this quote is to demonstrate the representation of 'sound' evidence and analysis for development policies. The articulation of how neutral or objective expert knowledge should be in guiding the regions develop polices and strategies obviously puts the experts (whether it is ESPON, OECD or NORDREGIO) in a very influential position. This expert knowledge of measuring, evaluating, comparing, and assessing, becomes the eyes and ears for regional policy makers to figure out where they are in the terrain of global competitiveness and if they are moving in the right direction. Through evaluation reports, benchmarking practices, and ranking systems, the regions can formulate and adjust development policies. The perceived necessity of this knowledge is illustrated in the quote below from a regional development plan:

The Värmland strategy includes 33 quantifiable objectives. The objectives are so-called impact goals on an overall community level. The various objectives are dependent on changes in economic conditions and what happens in the outside world. The quantifiable objectives constitute an important tool for finding out if we are moving in the right direction. Through continuously monitoring and measuring the development in Värmland, we can assess whether or not we need to reconsider some of the measures as we go along. It can for instance be a question of prioritizing certain activities above others. Knowing how Värmland is developing is also valuable for learning and gaining insight into the kind of efforts which benefit the region.

(41:6)

The position of neutral knowledge in regional development governance shows that the experts as evaluators have a crucial role not only for the ways that priorities are made but also for the way that legitimate knowledge is represented to have depoliticizing effects. The knowledge that concerns if a region is moving in the right direction is not produced by elected politicians and parties. Instead, the political goal of global competitiveness seems to be natural, transcending political debates, and the question whether or not the region is developing in a desired way is not an issue up for ideological scrutiny. On the contrary, this question has an objective answer provided by unbiased, neutral expertise through 'evidence based' assessments and evaluations resting on measurable variables of performance. This close connection between knowledge and objective truth makes it very difficult to raise concerns or criticize policy development from a position of political ideology.

In sum, the expert as a social actor is represented in two different ways or functions in the governing rationalities of regional development. The first is as producers and refers to highly skilled workers, researchers, and other creative people that in different ways can contribute to innovation and growth in the knowledge driven economy. The other representation is as evaluators and refers to policy experts that can render and deliver neutral knowledge that is needed for policy makers to navigate in the global terrain of competiveness. The experts are in both ways represented as very important to be successful in generating regional growth and developing strategies to maintain and foster success.

Global competiveness and its social actors

The way that social actors are represented in relation to regional development in the material makes it clear that the notion of global competiveness has a structuring significance for all of those representations. First of all, the region itself is a social actor in the global competition for resources, with the overarching rational goal to secure assets in order to survive, develop, and be prosperous. Furthermore, this also bestows a sense of meaning for how corporations, women, immigrants, and experts are represented in the material. Their particular role is represented in relation to their function for the region to be successful in this endeavor. Thus, by offering a hidden or future potential for competitiveness and growth in the case of women and immigrants, by contributing to innovations needed in order to compete or by supplying knowledge needed to navigate in policymaking the different subjects of expertise help out. In short, therefore, these are the social actors defined as important and given a specific subjectivity through the lens of global competitiveness.

One important aspect in understanding these representations of specific roles of social actors is the complexity of internal and external dynamics of the region in relation to global competitiveness. The region as an actor navigates and takes action in the global terrain to attract resources, such as people, capital, corporations, and other valuable assets that will benefit its growth and development. In this sense, the region is trying to interpret the preferences of these highly mobile resources. What will make a corporation settle down? What will make creative, highly skilled people want to move to the region? How can corporations be persuaded to relocate their knowledge-intense branches in the region? Internally, the region will try to govern the actors within the region in a way that meets those preferences, through restructuring living environments, in strategic programs for public-private coordination, as well as in cluster formations, and smart specialization. These dynamics gives a complex answer to the question 'for whom' the region is developed. The region should be transformed for actors outside of the region in order to meet their preferences, but the rationale for doing it is the survival and the development of those who inhabit the region. So, the priorities being made to be attractive for external actors are still made to secure the long run benefit, survival, and prosperity of internal actors.

Another important aspect, still related to the dynamic of internal and external, is how the articulations of global competitiveness construes specific representations of knowledge and expertise and how these representations produce specific stratifications of social actors. The subcategories of immigrants are one example. The need for experts to bring unbiased, neutral evidence based knowledge into policy formulation is another.

In closing: subjectivities for and of expertise

The complex dynamics that bring a specific meaning to social actors within regional development policies is a fundamental part of the grand narrative of regional development that was illustrated in Chapter 2. The shift into a threatening global terrain where regions compete for resources to survive and develop is the foundation for the overarching dynamic of internal and external logics that shapes the understanding of social actors in regional development. The social actors in the material can be divided in to three different kinds of subjectivities that relate to the grand narrative in different ways and play different roles in the endeavors of contemporary regional development.

The first kind we call *the desired*. The desired are social actors that are outside the region. They are part of the resources that regions struggle to attract. The desired are highly mobile on a global scale, ultra-rational actors with clearly formulated preferences for relocation. Where they locate will be based on if they see that a region can meet their preferences and objectives. The desired are the corporations, looking to maximize their profit and growth potential, bringing growth and prosperity to the region. They are also the highly skilled immigrants looking for an attractive living environment that can bring knowledge, corporations, and innovation into the region. The desired are continuously mobile and their preferences must continuously be met not to risk that they relocate to another region.

The second kind of subjectivities we label *the underdeveloped*. These are the social actors within the region that harbor a beneficial potential for growth and development. This potential of latent innovation and growth could be realized if they are given better circumstances to bloom. In order to do so the hurdles and thresholds that keep the potential back must be identified and strategically removed. This could be about overcoming low self-esteem or gaining knowledge needed to become more entrepreneurial and innovative, as the case of women, or about playing the role of increasing the attractiveness of the region for *the desired* by contributing to a requested service sector, as the case of low-skilled immigrants.

We label the third kind of subjectivity *the catalysts*. These are the social actors that are articulated with the role to navigate in the complex nexus of internal and external dynamics of regional development. The actors that formulate the strategies aim to interpret the external preferences and transform the internal resources in a way that will be attractive and competitive. Put short, the actors that can generate the needed knowledge and take necessary action to put the complex dynamics of regional development to work for innovation, growth, and prosperity. The regions as actors are given this role to play through a specific leadership that manages to transcend the ideological squabbling and form a united front in strategic actions to become globally competitive. In this regard, the evaluating experts play a crucial role as catalysts by producing the knowledge needed to formulate policy and strategies that help to navigate in the ongoing and harsh competition.

The type of subjectivities that emerge in the way that social actors in regional development are represented relates to expertise in different but nested ways. That being said, they all represent expertise that is needed in the region; for innovation, growth, knowledge production, navigation and policy development. At the same time they also legitimize a specific form of expertise for governing – the neutral, highly educated, ideologically un-biased, and innovative are traits in this regard. In other words, we are dealing with representations that articulate subjectivities of and for expertise in regional development.

6 Expertise and the (anti)political

Throughout this book we have pointed to how rationalities, technologies, and subjectivities in contemporary regional development come together in an assemblage that is affected by, as well as enables and sustains, certain articulations of expertise. We tried to chart this phenomenon not in terms of predetermined criteria for what constitutes expertise, but rather by illustrating how contemporary regional development lays out a grid of relations among subjects and objects where such expertise can take shape. In each of the chapters dealing with rationalities, technologies, and subjectivities, we have pointed to various ways in which the manifestation of expertise affects regional development today. In this final chapter of the book we aim to draw together some of those effects and focus on the overarching theme that we argue marks urban and regional development of our time, namely the processes of *depoliticization*. This means that we return to a discussion at a more abstract level, similar to the ones in the introductory chapter, as we consider the works of Chantal Mouffe (2005) in order to state what we mean by the term depoliticization. In addition, we also consider how governmentality scholars (Cruikshank, 1999; Li, 2007) can help explain and make sense of the ongoing processes where the assemblage of expertise can form in such ways that depoliticization is one of the prime effects. Finally, we end by briefly sketching what we see as a grim endpoint of a society so marked by struggles for competitiveness and depoliticization that it can be characterized as a *post-polis*.

Politics, the political, and depoliticization

In her influential works, alone and together with Ernesto Laclau, Chantal Mouffe has fashioned a post-structural take on the concepts of politics and the political (Laclau & Mouffe, 2001; Mouffe, 2005, 2013). For Mouffe, the starting point for dealing analytically with the political nature of social relations is to recognize this distinction between, on the one hand, *politics* and, on the other hand, *the political*. Put short, this means that she reserves the term politics to denote typical practices, objects, and subjects associated with the institutions of politics such as voting, debating, politicians, coalitions, strategies, parliaments, commissions, and policy formulation. The political, however, is a quality of the world at the level of ontology that capture how everything that come into being in social reality is contingent and conflictual or, in other words, how it is possible, but not necessary, that an object occupies the particular position in terms of meaning and understanding that it currently does. Mouffe (2005:9) articulates this distinction as follows:

> More precisely this is how I distinguish between 'the political' and 'politics': by 'the political' I mean the dimension of antagonism which I take to be constitutive of human societies, while by 'politics' I mean the set of practices and institutions through which an order is created, organizing human coexistence in the context of conflictuality provided by the political.

Hence, for Mouffe, the core of 'the political' is the conflictual reality of society; our different beliefs, understandings, views of reality, values, preferences, priorities, and reasons. The incredibly difficult but grave role for 'politics' is to manage these conflicts through different institutional settings in a way that prevents society from collapsing all together. This can be done either by acting out the conflicts through, for instance, deliberation and voting, consequently 'settling' the conflict, or through hiding and suppressing conflicts with the risky future consequences of letting them brew under the surface.

The way that regional leadership is represented in the empirical chapters of this book is a good example where the explicit strategy to suppress social conflicts rather than to address them is articulated. That is, the perceived need to look past 'ideological squabbling' in order to unite for global competiveness is articulating an awareness of underlying societal conflicts but arguing for a 'see nothing – hear nothing' approach. In Mouffe's terms, the ideological conflicts exist in the realm of 'the political' and the exclusion of those conflicts from the policy field of regional development happens in the realm of 'politics.' (Säll, 2014).

Another core message from Mouffe is to point to the risks and unethical dimensions of a too sharp separation of the realms of 'the political' and the realm of 'politics' through processes of depoliticization. She uses the concepts of 'antagonism' and 'agonism' to discuss these risks. Both terms denote the conflictual relationship between political opponents, but whereas the first refers to when opponents view each other as enemies, the second indicates a state where opponents view each other as adversaries. This is an important difference to keep in mind.

If social conflicts cannot be managed or acted out in a somewhat functional way through 'politics,' the risks include exclusion, collapsing cohesion and social integration, sharp polarization, political inequality, and a spreading disbelief in democracy and its institutions. The social conflicts will become antagonistic, or in other words, develop into a state where political opponents start to view each other as enemies, without any common ground and not acknowledging each other as legitimate political actors. The role of democracy is according to Mouffe to 'transform antagonism into agonism' (2005:20). The agonistic relationship is still conflictual but in a way where opponents acknowledge each other's legitimate right to participate and put forward their demands, where 'politics' is viewed as a functional arena to engage and act out social conflicts.

To keep the link between 'the political' and 'politics' vivid, the political institutions of society must, from Mouffe's perspective, recognize the contingent nature of meaning and knowledge. If perspectives, experiences, knowledge, and identities are systematically excluded from 'politics,' it threatens core values of democracy such as equality, justice and societal cohesion. The political dimensions of society – the social conflicts – can never be eradicated, but the capacity for 'politics' to manage the conflicts can be pushed back through depoliticization of those very conflicts.

We see Mouffe's concepts and analysis as an important framework for discussing the role of expertise in regional development as put forward in this book. The tendency to explicitly strategize to cover up ideological conflicts is not the only way that the contingent nature of meaning and knowledge is rejected throughout our analysis. The role and need for expertise for competitiveness in regional development is legitimized by assumptions about neutral, un-biased, transcendent knowledge for policy formulation.

Throughout this book we have analyzed this role of expertise in regional development, through its political rationalities, governmental technologies, and subjectivities. Just to remind how this 'neutral' knowledge of expertise is articulated, we would like to return to two illustrative examples from within the assemblage: those of *benchmarking* and *evaluation experts*.

In the case of benchmarking practices as governmental technologies a central feature is that they are not open for interpretation or ideological negotiation. The numerical devices of indexations and rankings are not produced with the intention to reflect and debate their value from different positions. They perform global and regional competition, make it tangible, provide 'neutral' information, and make it possible for regional policymakers to navigate, react, prioritize, and strategize to become a winner in the global competition. As knowledge, the 'neutral' nature of such expertise has a de-politicizing effect in the sense that it claims to transcend ideology, and it undermines the need for politicians to make ideological sense of the world. It detaches 'politics' from 'the political.'

In the case of the evaluation experts, the need for 'neutral' knowledge is connected to specific social actors rather than numerical devices – actors that have knowledge about how to interpret, strategize, and formulate policy accordingly to the mechanisms of global competiveness. In the same way, the knowledge that is articulated as needed in order to be successful in regional development is detached from political ideology and democratic representation. Instead it is 'evidence based,' resting on the use of indicators and continuous un-biased assessment.

Anti-politics and the will to improve

To sum up then, we argue that the presence of expertise contributes to what we call the processes of depoliticization. While Mouffe's work provides us with means to describe this state in contemporary regional development and its connection to expertise at an abstract level, we would also like to fashion a slightly more tangible account for the ways that these processes are maintained and expanded. Drawing on anthropologist Tania Murray Li (2007) and her ideas of 'the will to improve' helps us to do so.

For Li (2007), it is important to recognize that the presence of experts and expertise in governing has a clear tendency to render political problems non-political (or even anti-political) through technical procedures like the ones we have been describing in this book. In other words, while all governing rests on technical arrangements for realizing political ambitions and, in this sense, to materialize rule, a high presence of experts and expertise from outside of politics often sets into motion the processes of depoliticization that are hard to change:

> Questions that are rendered technical are simultaneously rendered non-political. For the most part, experts tasked with improvement exclude the structure of political-economic relations from their diagnoses and prescriptions. They focus more on the capacities of the poor than on the practices through which one social group impoverishes another. [...] A third dimension to improvement might also be labeled antipolitics: a design of programs as a deliberate measure to contain a challenge to the status quo.
>
> (Li, 2007:7f)

Nested in this technical rendering also lies a profound 'will to improve' among the experts, according to Li (2007). For us, this is an important point to make that we are not talking about an assemblage of expertise that is driven by some hidden agenda orchestrated by sinister agents. Rather, the actors involved here are probably (at least for the most part) working towards what the rationalities deem as improvements. In this case it means to foster competitiveness and to make a particular region a winner in the fierce global competition. In this sense, they work to improve the conditions of the object of governing, which in this particular case of course is regional development. That being said, the experts that enact the rationalities and produce various technologies quickly also become entrenched in this general logic of improvement. Thus, the people we trust to govern the development of any given domain of politics usually identify with whatever dominant rationalities that currently set out the basic assumptions for this governing. In this sense they become the trustees with respect to the rule they enact. When they get to work they do so meticulously and they try to advance the dominant rationalities precisely through their knowledge and expertise as they operate at a distance through subtile interventions and by structuring the conditions of possibility for rule in the domain:

> They [the trustees] desire to make the world better than what it is. Their methods are subtile. If they resort to violence, it is in the name of a higher good – the population at large, the survival of species, the stimulation of growth. Often, their schemes operate at a distance. They structure a field of possible actions. They modify processes. They entice and induce. They make certain courses of action easier or more difficult. Many schemes appear not as an external imposition, but as the natural expression of the everyday interactions of individuals and groups [...] Whatever the response, the claim to expertise in optimizing the lives of others is a claim to power, one that merits careful scrutiny.
>
> (Li, 2007:5)

With respect to regional development then, we are talking about a cadre of trustees that operate through their will to improve this domain according to the master rationality of competitiveness and the dominating narrative of new regionalism. As they do so they also work to instate a form of boundary between themselves as the legitimate trustees of this domain, and the subjects, practices, and objects that are the target of their rule. Thus, they are the ones who provide prescriptions, they are the ones who come up with solutions, and they are the ones who decide which path to take.

In addition, this will to improve often also spurs 'a will to empower' (Cruikshank, 1999) people or other social actors so as to help them overcome obstacles that hinder their full realization. In this book we have shown, for instance, how women and immigrants are examples of such social actors that the trustees work to empower along the lines of the dominant rationalities of regional development. Barbara Cruikshank (1999) discusses this in relation to the formation of democratic citizens and how they are shaped and formed. She calls this process *technologies of citizenship* and underscores how in neoliberal times this is a form of empowering that works by promoting freedom and the ability for people to help themselves:

> Technologies of citizenship operate according to a political rationality for governing people in ways that promote their autonomy, self-sufficiency, and political engagement; in the classic phrase of early philanthropists, they are intended to "help people to help themselves". This is a manner of governing that relies not on institutions, organized violence or state power but on securing the voluntary compliance of citizens. I argue, however, that the autonomy, interests, and wills of citizens are shaped as well as enlisted. [...] Democratic citizens, in short, are both the effects and the instruments of liberal governance.
>
> (Cruikshank, 1999:4)

As Cruikshank points out, while this is not a governing where power manifests as force or coercion, it is nevertheless the effects of power we are talking about. Indeed, from our point of view power is not just about force and coercion, but actually most of all about production. Power produces rationalities, technologies, and subjects, and it instates desires. Indeed, following Cruikshank's (1999) reasoning we argue that to focus solely on exclusions and dominations when one tries to understand power would be a mistake, precisely because it would miss the productive capacity of power. Thus, we view the social actors we detailed in Chapter 5 are accomplishments of power. They are vessels through which rationalities are able to operate and in terms of regional development the instalment of certain subjectivities is very important for the realization of the master rationality of competitiveness. Indeed, we could say that this rationality presupposes particular subjects. If they are not shaped in certain ways the rationality will not be able to uphold itself. Therefore, women and immigrants need to be empowered and included, not primarily because of democratic rights but rather because of their ability to help produce competitiveness.

We argue then, that as expertise intertwines with regional development it helps start and maintain the processes of depoliticization. Furthermore, an important part of explaining this lies in understanding the everyday work of those people directly involved with the assemblage of expertise, the trustees. Through their will to improve and will to empower according to the dominant rationalities they reproduce a social order where politics and the political is subsumed under claims of and for expert knowledge. In the case of regional development we argue that this is a very powerful part of the rationalities that guide its governing. Indeed, it is so powerful that this expertise often makes claims that transform political orders into natural ones.

Post-polis and chrematistics

To furnish the final remark concerning what we have shown throughout this book we find it important to stop for a moment and ask ourselves what kind of society, community, or *polis* that could exist under such rationalities that we have identified dominant within regional development. Doing so, we argue, allows us to sketch the contours of where we might be heading if we continue down the path of the warlike rationalities of competition and competitiveness. To be sure, when doing so we do not claim to represent an order that is soon to be fully realized (perhaps not even one that is very likely). Rather, by ideal type reasoning we can lay bare some of the inherent traits in the dominant rationalities of contemporary regional development and its displacement of politics for expertise.

Geographers Mekonnen Tesfahuney and Katarina Schough (2009) provide such an ideal type representation that is usable for us here when they theorize the differences between, on the one hand, *polis*, a conception of a political community with its roots in the classic city state in Ancient Greece and

Aristotelian reasoning, and, on the other hand, what they call *post-polis*. In their conception, the post-polis is a modern manifestation of a political community (the city, the region, etc.) that to great extent resembles the one ruled by the rationalities, technologies, and subjects that we have described here.

First off then, following Tesfahuney and Schough (2009) there is a stark contrast between the economic regimes that traditionally guide the political community of polis and those that operate in post-polis. By departing from a distinction between *oikonomía* (the art of managing the household) and *chrematistics* (the art of moneymaking and commerce) that originally occurs in Aristoteles (2003) and that has been further developed by Derrida (1992), Tesfahuney and Schough (2009) classify the community of polis as one where the economy is geared towards the household with the aim of living and living well. With oikonomía as an axiom, polis provides through planning and maintaining production within boundaries for what its people need. Wealth is measured according to use-value logics and it is subordinated under the general good of the household and the community (polis). Chrematistics also has a role to play in polis in the form of commerce and trade that enable households to acquire the needs that they cannot produce themselves by trading with people and communities nearby. Thus, the *agora* (the town square) fills an important economic function; however, in polis, this function is continuously up for discussion in terms of the limits for commerce in relation to the needs of the public. In other words, chrematistics is a form of second order economic logic that is subordinate to oikonomía in polis. In post-polis this relationship is fundamentally altered.

Indeed, Aristoteles (2003) actually defines a difference between two forms of chrematistics where the first form is the one that functions as a supplemental logic to that of oikonomía mentioned above. The second, however, is a version that has lost its connection to the household and where 'the art of moneymaking' has become an end in and of itself (Stahel, 2006). As such, in contrast to oikonomía, chrematistics operates without limits and boundaries. Rather, it is a logic that extends itself to all areas of social life, and wherever it can, it will impose a thinking of interest, equivalents, and return on investment. For Tesfahuney and Schough (2009), this is a telling trait for post-polis, a community marked by an economic order that fundamentally has no external reference point beyond just 'more growth of money' as a form of legitimation. Indeed, whereas polis has been, over time, founded on a logic of rule that variously has found its legitimation in God, heritage, land or people, post-polis ultimately needs no such legitimation beyond the capacity to generate growth.

In terms of people and inhabitants, polis, in its range of historical expressions, has had complex relations in place. However, in its Aristotelian notion, and later with the rise of liberal democracies, it has generally operated on the assumption that humans are political animals that need political orders though which they can organize life. Thus, the inhabitants of polis are *citizens* and later also *individuals*. Indeed, in most modern democracies individuals and citizens are tracked and instated through personal identification numbers (social security, etc.) that tie them to rights and obligations. Post-polis, on the other hand, is a community where the inhabitants are consumers, entrepreneurs, and risk-taking speculative subjects that continuously act in accordance with chrematistics. Thus they come to life and take part of society, not through a personal identification number, but rather through a credit card number (Tesfahuney & Schough, 2009). They form relations and enter into agreement only as long as they see such relations profitable for their investments.

Finally, in terms of governing, and of importance for the points we make in this book, post-polis is an order where political governing has been exchanged for the technocratic rule of expertise. Politics, in post-polis, has been reduced to an endeavor where expertise works to identify problems and then sets out to remedy them on neutral grounds. However, this neutrality is firmly situated in chrematistic logics. While biopolitics and means for optimizing the public is the goal in polis as well as post-polis, the latter works through technologies that help produce a continuous surveillance of more or less all aspects of human life. This is possible in post-polis since chrematistics have no limits. Thus, with the rise of big data and new advanced tracking systems as well as readily available biometrical devices (face recognition, finger prints, etc.) the full financialization of human life is a horizon within reach in post-polis.

So, in terms of economic registers, in the production of subjects as well as in the forms of control and governing, polis and post-polis expressed as ideal types are two sharply distinct and different communities. In addition, we could go on and mention how they have different expressions in space (manifested in different architectural ideals), how they operate on competing accounts of time, how they articulate different moral codexes, and how they build on contrasting views on the role and function of knowledge. Yet, at this point it is enough to simply state a basic property concerning post-polis. Along all these dimensions it follows the logic of chrematistics where the overarching purpose is the already mentioned never ending quest for more money.

In other words, this post-political representation has an eerie resemblance with the assumptions that underpin the dominant logics of contemporary regional development as we have detailed them in this book. Chrematistics here takes the form of unending growth and competitiveness. Indeed, growth in itself is not enough; rather, it is growth *rates* that function as a measure of success in the competition that matters.

Thus, we argue that as the rationalities, technologies, and subjects of regional development interchange with expertise in the ways we have tried to describe here, they produce a vision and a trajectory that points in the direction of a post-polis.

What is more, as this happens and politics is removed from the decision making process, there is a tendency for this order to inscribe processes and events as necessary, natural phenomena rather than the end results of precisely political processes.

In his lectures at *College de France* Foucault (2007, 2008) described such naturalizations that he found to be associated with the emergence of advance liberal rule as *veridiction*. As an example he uses the spread of market practices and market thinking to all domains of society. Not only is the market then imposed upon domains where it did not usually operate, but its legitimation is also gradually removed from the realm of law, regulation, and judicial power to the realm of nature and natural order.

Importantly, the assemblage of expertise function in such a way it enables a mobile form of rule that is remarkably versatile in terms of its capacity to travel from context to context and install itself as part of local circumstances. While regional development is institutionally diverse around the world (even in the EU) it is our experience that the expertise can find ways to translate local claims, goals, and ambitions to work along, or at least not in opposition to its most important rationalities, technologies, and subjects. Ong and Collier (2005) classify such mobile and traveling assemblages as *global*. By doing so they denote a certain set of assemblages where elements of their composition are easy to lift and recombine with new ones in new circumstances. The global assemblage of expertise in this sense *reaches into* local contexts around the world and codes them, structures them, and is often successful in translating between them. Thus, such *global forms* (Ong & Collier, 2005) are available to trustees working in local context, and they can draw on a vast register of expertise to install the components they need at the time as they work to guide and steer their region towards competitiveness.

What the future holds?

Given that the assemblage of expertise that we have detailed in this book is precisely such a mobile and versatile one, it makes sense to end things here by briefly pointing out two main directions that we think will be important for understanding its development in the years to come. Of course, this does not mean that other things are not important or that these two areas are not already in effect. Rather, they are what we would call important new avenues for research for anyone who wants to understand expertise as well as regional development in the near future. Indeed, we have already touched upon these aspects in different circumstances as we have been discussing rationalities, technologies, and subjectivities; however, this is our way of underlining the importance of *robotic expertise* and *consultancy* in the regional development of tomorrow.

Beginning with robotic expertise we argue that the rise of Big Data, algorithmic decision making, and artificial intelligence (AI) represents an important shift and opportunity for expertise in regional development. Indeed, it is also a shift that seems likely to further the tendencies of depoliticization and contribute to the formation of a post-polis. Here we will not draw out the lines of this reasoning very far, however, suffice to say that scholars that have started to investigate some of the expressions of knowledge and expertise that arise as part of this development have pointed to a range of effects (Amoore & Piotukh, 2015; Mayer-Schönberger & Cukier, 2014). First then, while, for instance, algorithms and big data can help with decision making, they are not neutral and objective ways of knowing reality. Rather, the algorithms must be created and enacted by forms of expertise. All such algorithms that aspire to aid in governing processes are programmed according to dominating rationalities and what they offer is not so much neutral and objective decision making as the illusion of it (Hansen, 2015). In other words, as cities and regions are starting to adopt SMART systems of governing, the decision making associated with these is still very much a matter of power and politics (eg. Lesczynski, 2016). Importantly though, the advent of big data, algorithms, and AI promises to move expertise calculations out of the realm of probabilities into a more deterministic account of not only what has happened, but also what is going to happen in the future (Amoore, 2013). This, we argue, will be something to keep a close eye on in the years to come.

Another important trajectory for future research is to study the *developing market for policy consultancy* related to regional development. In this book, we have described and discussed the travelling expertise in regional development and how this mode of governing can be seen as depoliticized and depoliticizing in the sense that political representation and ideological conflicts are articulated as obsolete. Related to this development we see a growing importance and use of private consultants in regional policy processes. Consultants are hired as neutral non-ideological experts both to give input for strategic navigation and policy formulation and in the role as neutral evaluators to measure performance. The depoliticized mode of governing is thus merging public policy with the market in a way that runs deeper than outscoring specific tasks or drawing inspiration from the private sector as described in the NPM literature. It entails a true hybridization of the market and 'politics' in the sense that the demanded 'neutral' policy knowledge becomes a commodity and the relationship between knowledge production, political decision making and evaluation merges the work of elected assemblies and private consultancy firms in a very concrete way. The mutual interdependence between 'politics' and consultancy firms in regional development raises serious questions about the state of democratic legitimacy and political accountability within the field of regional development, and it also raises questions about power relations and dynamics in this hybridized mode of governing.

In the literature on *policy consultants* (cf. Howlett & Migone, 2013a, 2013b, 2013c, 2014) the main argument has been that governance today calls for new understandings of how policy advice is 'arranged' in a policy advisory system with less clear boundaries between such dichotomies as public and private. Policy consultants denote a broader category of actors whose expertise directly rivals that of traditional bureaucrats in many ways. As such, they indicate a new modality of consultants and their prevalence has been linked, among other things, to the 'audit society' (Power, 1997) and the need for evidence based policy making (Saint-Martin, 1998, 2000). An inter-related strand of research that is of particular importance for these analyses has emerged during the last decade where the broader theme has been the mobile character of policy and policy experts, and where more specific accounts have been directed towards policy consultants as vehicles for policy (McCann & Ward, 2012; Peck & Theodore, 2015). Within the field there is an explicit interest in the shifting of political decisions to arenas that are less subject to democratic norms, practices and oversight; the privileging of business models and market principles, and a reshaping of the processes and practices through which policies are developed and assessed (Prince, 2012).

On this note, we end this book by hoping that in the future more research will be devoted to these new and emerging effects of expertise in regional development. We are certain that this is important for understanding the way that urban- and regional development will continue to advance in the years to come. We also think that for scholars interested in expertise more generally, this policy field could prove particularly interesting. To paraphrase Foucault (1984:343), we are not saying that everything is bad; however, we are saying that everything is potentially dangerous. Dangerous things deserve the attention of critical scholarship.

Appendix 1
Empirical illustrations

The following is a list of sources used in the empirical illustrations throughout the book. As we explain and develop further in the text, these sources are part of a large dataset comprising documents, interviews, surveys, films, websites, images, and observations generated as part of multiple different research projects. References in the book utilize the numbers listed here rather than the title and/or producer.

No	Producer	Title	Year
01	Landstinget i Värmland	Utredning om Värmlands framtida regiontillhörighet	2008
02	Swedish government: Ministry of industry, employment and communication	Nationell strategi för regional tillväxt och attraktionskraft 2014–2020	2014
03	ESPON (European observation network for territorial development and cohesion)	Spatial indicators for a Europe 2020 territorial analysis: SIESTA (Final report)	2013
04	NMC (The Nordic Council of Ministers)	Global Pressure – Nordic solutions? The Nordic Globalization Barometer 2010	2010
05	Region Dalarna	Dalastrategin – Dalarna 2020	2014
06	OECD (The Organization for Economic Cooperation and Development)	OECD Territorial Reviews Sweden	2010
07	Regionförbundet Södra Småland	Mötesplats södra Småland – Regionalt utvecklingsprogram, en strategi för Kronobergs län.	2009
08	SWECO	Hur står sig en Västsvensk region?	2010
09	Landstinget i Värmland	Värmland egen region	2010

(Continued)

No	Producer	Title	Year
10	European Union	The Territorial State and Perspectives of the European Union: Background Document for the Territorial Agenda of the European Union 2020	2011
11	European commission	Smart specialisation platform - What is smart specialisation? https:// s3platform.jrc.ec.europa.eu/ what-is-smart-specialisation-2019-10-15	2019
12	European commission	Smart specialisation platform – Smart specialisation in practice https://s3platform.jrc.ec.europa.eu/ what-is-smart-specialisation-2019-10-15	2019
13	United nations	Sustainable development goals Knowledge platform – Sustainable development goal 5: Target and indicators https:// sustainabledevelopment.un.org/sdg5 2019-10-15	2019
14	OECD	OECD Regional development policy https://www.oecd.org/regional/ regionaldevelopment.htm 2019-10-15	2019
15	OECD	OECD Regional wellbeing https://www.oecdregionalwellbeing.org/ 2019-10-15	2019
16	OECD	OECD Regional wellbeing – lower Saxony https://www.oecdregionalwellbeing.org/ DE9.html 2019-10-15	2019
17	NORDREGIO	Regional potential index 2017 https://www.nordregio.org/maps/regional-potential-index-2017/ 2019-10-15	2019
18	Swedish government	Ny rapport: Norden starkt med Stockholm i täten https://www.regeringen.se/ artiklar/2018/02/state-of-the-nordic-region-norden-starkt-med-stockholm-i-taten/ 2019-10-15	2019
19	NORDREGIO	The purpose of the regional potential index https://archive.nordregio.se/Metameny/ Nordregio-News/2016/State-of-the-Nordic-region-2016/The-purpose-of-the-Regional-Potential-Index/index. html 2019-10-15	2019
20	Region Jämtland-Härjedalen	Innovation program of region Jämtland-Härjedalen 2020	2016
21	Reglab/Kontigo (Lindqvist & Kempinsky)	Innovationsindex 2015 – Regional förmåga till ekonomisk förnyelse	2016
22	Xunta De Galicia Consellería de Economía e Industria	Smart specialisation strategy in Galicia 2014–2020	2014
23	Region Syddanmark	Regional væxt- og udviklingsstrategi – Det gode liv som væxtskaber 2016–2019	2016
24	Regionförbundet Sörmland	Sörmlandsstrategin 2020	2013

No	Producer	Title	Year
25	European commission – Directorate General for Regional and Urban Policy	Partners	2014
26	Globaliseringsrådet	Expert report no. 8 Du sköna nya globaliserade värld? Starka klusters och svaga regioners betydelse för ekonomisk tillväxt	2008
27	OECD	OECD Territorial Reviews Skåne, Sweden	2012
28	Ansvarskommittén	Regional utveckling och regional samhällsorganisation SOU 2007:13	2007
29	Sveriges kommuner och landsting	Bilda fler och storskaliga regioner: Sverige behöver fler starka tillväxtregioner	2011
30	ESPON	Territorial Scenarios and Visions for Europe	2014
31	Region Örebro	Utvecklingsstrategi för Örebroregionen	2010
32	Globaliseringsforum	Report 4 – Sverige som kunskapsnation – Klarar sig näringslivet utan storföretagen?	2012
33	Attraktionskraft Sverige	Service – En förutsättning för tillväxt	2014
34	Region Västerbotten	Regional utvecklingsstrategi för Västerbottens län 2014–2020	2013
35	Region Dalarna	Dalastrategin – Dalarna 2020	2014
36	The Swedish Government	Handlingsplan för jämställd regional tillväxt	2012
37	Regionförbundet i Kalmar län	Regional utvecklingsstrategi för Kalmar län 2012–2020	2012
38	ESPON (European Observation Network for Territorial Development and Cohesion)	Territorial Impact of Globalization for Europe and its Regions: TIGER	2013
39	Attraktionskraft Sverige	Fact-sheet	2014
40	Region Jönköping	Regional utvecklingsstrategi för region Jönköping 2025	2013
41	Region Värmland	Värmlandsstrategin 2014–2020	2014

Bibliography

Acuto, M., & Curtis, S. (2013). *Reassembling international theory: Assemblage thinking and international relations.* Houndsmill, Basingstoke, Hampshire; New York: Palgrave Pivot.

Alonso, W., & Starr, P. (1987). *The politics of numbers.* New York: Russell Sage Foundation for the National Committee for Research on the 1980 Census.

Amoore, L. (2013). *The politics of possibility: Risk and security beyond probability.* Durham, NC: Duke University Press Books.

Amoore, L., & Piotukh, V. (Eds.). (2015). *Algorithmic life: Calculative devices in the age of big data* (1st ed.). London; New York: Routledge.

Aristoteles. (2003). *Politiken.* Sävedalen: Åström.

Austin, J. L. (1976). *How to do things with words: The William James lectures delivered at Harvard university in 1955.* Oxford: Oxford University Press.

Bacchi, C. (2009). *Analysing policy: what's the problem represented to be?* Frenchs Forest, N.S.W.: Pearson.

Bacchi, C. (2012). Why study problematizations? Making politics visible. *Open Journal of Political Science, 02*(01), 1–8.

Bacchi, C., & Goodwin, S. (2016). *Poststructural policy analysis: A guide to practice* (1st ed.). New York: Palgrave Pivot.

Bache, I. (2007). *Europeanization and multilevel governance: Cohesion policy in the European Union and Britain.* Lanham, MD: Rowman & Littlefield Publishers.

Barad, K. M. (2007). *Meeting the universe halfway: Quantum physics and the entanglement of matter and meaning.* Durham, NC: Duke University Press.

Brenner, N. (2004). *New state spaces: Urban governance and the rescaling of statehood.* Oxford; New York: Oxford University Press.

Bristow, G. (2005). Everyone's a 'winner': Problematising the discourse of regional competitiveness. *Journal of Economic Geography, 5*(3), 285–304.

Bruno, I. (2009). The "indefinite discipline" of competitiveness benchmarking as a neoliberal technology of government. *Minerva, 47*(3), 261–280.

Butler, J. (1990). *Gender trouble: Feminism and the subversion of identity.* New York: Routledge.

Butler, J. (1993). *Bodies that matter: On the discursive limits of "sex."* New York: Routledge.

Callon, M. (Ed.). (1998). *Laws of the markets* (1st ed.). Oxford; Malden, MA: Wiley-Blackwell.

Cerny, P. G. (1997). Paradoxes of the competition state: The dynamics of political globalization. *Government and Opposition, 32*(02), 251–274.

Cerny, P. G. (1999). Globalization and the erosion of democracy. *European Journal of Political Research, 36*(1), 1–26.

Cooke, P. (1992). Regional innovation systems: Competitive regulation in the new Europe. *Geoforum, 23*(3), 365–382.

Cooke, P., Heidenreich, M., & Braczyk, H. J. (2004). *Regional innovation systems: The role of governance in a globalised world* (Vol. 363–388). London: Routledge.

Cox, K. R. (2009). 'Rescaling the state' in question. *Cambridge Journal of Regions, Economy and Society, 2*(1), 107–121.

Cruikshank, B. (1999). *The will to empower: Democratic citizens and other subjects* (1st ed.). Ithaca, NY: Cornell University Press.

Dean, M. (2010). *Governmentality: Power and rule in modern society.* Thousand Oaks, CA: SAGE Publications.

DeLanda, M. (2016). *Assemblage theory* (1st ed.). Edinburgh: Edinburgh University Press.

Deleuze, G., & Guattari, F. (2004). *A thousand plateaus: Capitalism and Schizophrenia.* London: Continuum.

Deleuze, G., & Guattari, F. (2009). *Anti-oedipus: Capitalism and Schizophrenia.* New York: Penguin Classics.

Deleuze, G., & Parnet, C. (2007). *Dialogues II.* New York: Columbia University Press.

Derrida, J. (1992). *Given time. 1, Counterfeit money.* Chicago, IL: University of Chicago Press.

Desrosières, A. (2014). *The politics of large numbers: A history of statistical reasoning.* Cambridge, MA: Harvard University Press.

Dicken, P. (2011). *Global shift: mapping the changing contours of the world economy* (6th ed.). Thousand Oaks, CA: Sage.

Elden, S. (2007). Governmentality, calculation, territory. *Environment and Planning D: Society and Space, 25*(3), 562–580.

Erkkilä, T., & Piironen, O. (2014). Shifting fundaments of European higher education governance: Competition, ranking, autonomy and accountability. *Comparative Education, 50*(2), 177–191.

Espeland, W. N., & Sauder, M. (2007). Rankings and reactivity: How public measures recreate social worlds. *American Journal of Sociology, 113*(1), 1–40.

Espeland, W. N., & Stevens, M. L. (2008). A sociology of quantification. *European Journal of Sociology / Archives Européennes de Sociologie, 49*(03), 401–436.

Esposito, E., & Stark, D. (2019). What's observed in a rating? Rankings as orientation in the face of uncertainty. *Theory, Culture & Society, 36*(4), 3–26. doi:10.1177/0263276419826276.

Fawn, R. (2009). 'Regions' and their study: Wherefrom, what for and whereto? *Review of International Studies, 35*(Supplement S1), 5–34.

Florida, R.L. (2002). *The rise of the creative class: and how it's transforming work, leisure, community and everyday life.* New York: Basic Books.

Flyvbjerg, B. (2006). Five misunderstandings about case-study research. *Qualitative Inquiry, 12*(2), 219–245.

Forsberg, G., & Lindgren, G. (2010). *Nätverk och skuggstrukturer i regionalpolitiken.* Karlstad: Karlstad University Press.

Foucault, M. (1980). *Power/knowledge: Selected interviews and other writings, 1972–1977* (First American Edition, Stained; C. Gordon, Ed.). New York: Vintage.

Foucault, M. (1984). On the genealogy of ethics: An overview of work in progress. In P. Rabinow (Ed.), *The Foucault reader* (pp. 340–372). New York: Pantheon.

Foucault, M. (1991). *Discipline and punish: The birth of the prison.* Harmondsworth: Penguin.

Foucault, M. (2007). *Security, territory, population* (2009 edition; A. I. Davidson, Ed.; G. Burchell, Trans.). Basingstoke: Palgrave Macmillan.

Foucault, M. (2008). *The birth of biopolitics: Lectures at the Collège de France, 1978–1979* (1st ed.). New York: Picador.

Fougner, T. (2006). The state, international competitiveness and neoliberal globalisation: Is there a future beyond? *Review of International Studies, 32*(01), 165–185.

Giannone, D. (2017). The politics of global indicators in designing, promoting and legitimating the competition state. *Partecipazione e conflitto, 10*(2), 472–491.

Glass, M. R., & Rose-Redwood, R. (2014). *Performativity, politics, and the production of social space.* New York: Routledge.

Glynos, J., & Howarth, D. (2007). *Logics of critical explanation in social and political theory.* London: Routledge.

Hacking, I. (1991). How Should We Do the History of Statistics. In: G. Burchell, C. Gordon, & P. Miller (Eds.), *The Foucault Effect: Studies in Governmentality With Two Lectures By and An Interview With Michel Foucault* (pp. 181–195). Chicago: The University of Chicago Press.

Hacking, I. (2006). *The emergence of probability: A philosophical study of early ideas about probability, induction and statistical inference.* Cambridge, UK: Cambridge University Press.

Hansen, H. K. (2015). Numerical operations, transparency illusions and the datafication of governance. *European Journal of Social Theory, 18*(2), 203–220.

Hansen, H. K., & Flyverbom, M. (2015). The politics of transparency and the calibration of knowledge in the digital age. *Organization, 22*(6), 872–889.

Hansen, H. K., & Porter, T. (2012). What do numbers do in transnational governance? *International Political Sociology, 6*(4), 409–426.

Harrison, J. (2006). Re-reading the new regionalism: A sympathetic critique. *Space and Polity, 10*(1), 21–46.

Harvey, D. (1989). From managerialism to entrepreneurialism: The transformation in urban governance in late capitalism. *Geografiska Annaler. Series B, Human Geography, 71*(1), 3–17.

Higgins, V., & Larner, W. (2010). *Calculating the social: Standards and the reconfiguration of governing.* Basingstoke, Hampshire: Palgrave Macmillan.

Hooghe, L., Marks, G., & Schakel, A. H. (2010). *The rise of regional authority: A comparitive study of 42 democracies.* London: Routledge.

Hörnström, L. (2010). *Redistributive regionalism: Narratives on regionalisation in the Nordic periphery.* Ume\aa: Statsvetenskapliga institutionen, Umeå universitet.

Howarth, D. R. R. (2013). *Poststructuralism and after: Structure, subjectivity and power.* New York: Palgrave Macmillan.

Howlett, M., & Migone, A. (2013a). Policy advice through the market: The role of external consultants in contemporary policy advisory systems. *Policy and Society, 32*(3), 241–254.

Howlett, M., & Migone, A. (2013b). Searching for substance: Externalization, politicization and the work of Canadian policy consultants 2006–2013. *Central European Journal of Public Policy, 7*(1), 112–133.

Howlett, M., & Migone, A. (2013c). The permanence of temporary services: The reliance of Canadian federal departments on policy and management consultants. *Canadian Public Administration, 56*(3), 369–390.

Howlett, M., & Migone, A. (2014). Assessing contract policy work: Overseeing Canadian policy consultants. *Public Money & Management, 34*(3), 173–180.

Jäger, S., & Maier, F. (2009). Theoretical and methodological aspects of Foucauldian critical discourse analysis. In R. Wodak & M. Meyer (Eds.), *Methods of critical discourse analysis* (2nd ed.) (pp. 34–61). Los Angeles, CA: SAGE Publications Ltd.

Jessop, B. (2002). *The future of the capitalist state* (1st ed.). Cambridge, UK; Malden, MA: Polity.

Jessop, B. (2015). The course, contradictions, and consequences of extending competition as a mode of (meta-)governance: Towards a sociology of competition and its limits. *Distinktion: Journal of Social Theory, 16*(2), 167–185.

Jones, M., & MacLeod, G. (1999). Towards a regional renaissance? Reconfiguring and rescaling England's economic governance. *Transactions of the Institute of British Geographers, 24*(3), 295–313.

Jones, M., & MacLeod, G. (2004). Regional spaces, spaces of regionalism: Territory, insurgent politics and the English question. *Transactions of the Institute of British Geographers, 29*(4), 433–452.

Jorgensen, M. W., & Phillips, L. J. (2002). *Discourse analysis as theory and method* (1st ed.). London: SAGE Publications Ltd.

Keating, M. (1998). *The new regionalism in Western Europe: Territorial restructuring and political change.* Cheltenham: Edward Elgar.

Keating, M. (2003). The invention of regions: Political restructuring and territorial government in Western Europe. In N. Brenner (Ed.), *State/space: A reader* (pp. 256–277). Malden, MA: Blackwell Pub.

Keating, M. (2013). *Rescaling the European state: The making of territory and the rise of the meso.* Oxford: Oxford University Press.

Kress, G. R., & Van Leeuwen, T. (2006). *Reading images: The grammar of visual design.* London: Routledge.

Lacan, J. (2018). *The four fundamental concepts of psycho-analysis.* New York: Routledge.

Laclau, E., & Mouffe, C. (2001). *Hegemony and socialist strategy: Towards a radical democratic politics.* London; New York: Verso.

Larner, W., & Le Heron, R. (2002). The spaces and subjects of a globalising economy: A situated exploration of method. *Environment and Planning D: Society and Space, 20*(6), 753–774.

Latour, B. (1987). *Science in action: How to follow scientists and engineers through society.* Cambridge, MA: Harvard University Press.

Latour, B. (2005). *Reassembling the social: An introduction to actor-network-theory.* Oxford; New York: Oxford University Press.

Law, J., & Mol, A. (2002). *Complexities: Social studies of knowledge practices.* Durham, NC: Duke University Press.

Leszczynski, A. (2016). Speculative futures: Cities, data, and governance beyond smart urbanism. *Environment and Planning A, 48*(9), 1691–1708.

Lobao, L., Martin, R., & Rodríguez-Pose, A. (2009). Editorial: Rescaling the state: New modes of institutional–territorial organization. *Cambridge Journal of Regions, Economy and Society, 2*(1), 3–12.

Loughlin, J. (2007). Reconfiguring the state: Trends in territorial governance in European states. *Regional & Federal Studies, 17*(4), 385.

Lovering, J. (1999). Theory led by policy: The inadequacies of the "new regionalism" (Illustrated from the case of wales). *International Journal of Urban and Regional Research, 23*(2), 379–395.

Mansfield, N. (2000). *Subjectivity: Theories of the self from Freud to Haraway.* New York: New York University Press.

Mayer-Schönberger, V., & Cukier, K. (2014). *Big data: A revolution that will transform how we live, work, and think* (Reprint edition). Boston, MA: Eamon Dolan/Mariner Books.

McCann, E., & Ward, K. (2012). Policy assemblages, mobilities and mutations: Toward a multidisciplinary conversation. *Political Studies Review, 10*(3), 325–332.

Miller, P., & Rose, N. (2008). *Governing the present: Administering economic, social and personal life.* Cambridge, UK: Polity.

Mitander, T. (2015). *Regio ex machina: Om det regionala medborgarskapets villkor.* Karlstad: Karlstad University Press.

Mitander, T., Säll, L., & Öjehag-Pettersson, A. (Eds.). (2013). *Det regionala samhällsbyggandets praktiker. Tiden, makten, rummet.* Göteborg: Bokförlaget Daidalos.

Mol, A. (2002). *The body multiple: Ontology in medical practice.* Durham, NC: Duke University Press Books.

Mouffe, C. (2005). *On the political* (1st ed.). London; New York: Routledge.

Mouffe, C. (2013). *Agonistics: Thinking the world politically.* London: Verso.

Murray Li, T. (2007). *The will to improve: Governmentality, development, and the practice of politics.* Durham, NC: Duke University Press Books.

Newman, J., & Clarke, J. (2009). *Publics, politics and power: Remaking the public in public services.* Los Angeles, CA; London: SAGE.

Ohmae, K. (1993). The rise of the region state. *Foreign Affairs, 72*(2), 78–87.

Ohmae, K. (1996). *End of the nation state: The rise of regional economies.* London: HarperCollins.

Öjehag-Pettersson, A. (2015). *Space craft: Globalization and governmentality in regional development.* Karlstad: Karlstad University Press.

Öjehag-Pettersson, A. (2017). Working for change: Projectified politics and gender equality. *NORA – Nordic Journal of Feminist and Gender Research, 25*(3), 163–178.

Öjehag-Pettersson, A. (2019). Measuring innovation space: Numerical devices as governmental technologies. *Territory, Politics, Governance, 0*(0), 1–18.

Ong, A., & Collier, S. J. (Eds.). (2005). *Global assemblages: Technology, politics, and ethics as anthropological problems* (1st ed.). Malden, MA: Wiley-Blackwell.

Paasi, A. (2009). The resurgence of the 'region' and 'regional identity': Theoretical perspectives and empirical observations on regional dynamics in Europe. *Review of International Studies, 35*(Supplement S1), 121–146.

Peck, J. (2002). Political economies of scale: Fast policy, interscalar relations, and neoliberal workfare. *Economic Geography, 78*(3), 331–360.

Peck, J. (2005). Struggling with the creative class. *International Journal of Urban and Regional Research, 29*(4), 740–770.

Peck, J., & Tickell, A. (1994). Searching for a new institutional fix: The after-fordist crisis and the global-local disorder. In A. Amin (Ed.), *Post-fordism: A Reader* (pp. 280–315). Oxford: Blackwell.

Peck, J., & Tickell, A. (2002). Neoliberalizing space. *Antipode, 34*(3), 380–404.

Porter, M. E. (1990). *The competitive advantage of nations.* London: Macmillan.

Porter, M. E. (1998). Clusters and the new economics of competition. *Harvard Business Review, 76*(6) (November/December), 77–90.

Porter, T. (2012). Making serious measures: Numerical indices, peer review, and transnational actor-networks. *Journal of International Relations and Development,* *15*(4), 532–557.

Power, M. (1997). *The audit society: Rituals of verification.* Oxford: Oxford University Press.

Prince, R. (2012). Policy transfer, consultants and the geographies of governance. *Progress in Human Geography, 36*(2), 188–203.

Rhodes, R. A. W. (1994). The ollowing out of the state: The changing nature of the public service in Britain. *The Political Quarterly, 65*(2), 138–151.

Rinehart, J. (1995). The ideology of competitiveness. *Monthly Review: An Independent Socialist Magazine, 47*(5), 14.

Rönnblom, M. (2008). Var tog politiken vägen? Om regionalpolitik, jämställdhet och statens förändrade former. *Tidskrift För Genusvetenskap, 28*(1), 30–53.

Rose, G. (2016). *Visual methodologies: An introduction to researching with visual materials.* London: Sage.

Rose, N. (1991). Governing by numbers: Figuring out democracy. *Accounting, Organizations and Society, 16*(7), 673–692.

Saint-Martin, D. (1998). Management consultants, the state, and the politics of administrative reform in Britain and Canada. *Administration & Society, 30*(5), 533–568.

Saint-Martin, D. (2000). *Building the new managerialist state: Consultants and the politics of public sector reform in comparative perspective.* Oxford: Oxford University Press.

Säll, L. (2012). *Clusters as theory and politics: The discursive practices of regional growth policy.* Karlstad: Karlstad University Press.

Säll, L. (2014). *Regionalpolitikens diskursiva grunder och gränser: Om politik, makt och kunskap i det regionala samhällsbyggandet.* Karlstad: Karlstad University Press.

Stahel, A. W. (2006). Complexity, oikonomía and political economy. *Ecological Complexity, 3*(4), 369–381.

Stimson, R. J., Stough, R. R., & Roberts, B. H. (2002). *Regional economic development: Analysis and planning strategy.* Berlin Heidelberg: Springer-Verlag.

Stockholm mest dynamiska regionen i Norden enligt ny rapport. (2018, February 8). Retrieved October 15, 2019, from DN.SE website: https://www.dn.se/sthlm/stockholm-mest-dynamiska-regionen-i-norden-enligt-ny-rapport/

Storper, M. (1997). *The regional world: Territorial development in a global economy (Perspectives on economic change).* New York: The Guilford Press.

Syssner, J. (2006). *What kind of regionalism?* (1st ed.). Frankfurt am Main: Peter Lang GmbH.

Tesfahuney, M., & Schough, K. (2009). Postpolis. In G. Graninger & C. Knuthammar (Eds.), *Samhällsbyggande och integration: Frågor om assimilation, mångfald och boende: Vols* (pp. 119–148). Linköping: Linköping University Electronic Press.

Tiebout, C. M. (1956). A pure theory of local expenditures. *Journal of Political Economy, 64*(5), 416–424.

van Leeuwen, T. (2007). Legitimation in discourse and communication. *Discourse & Communication, 1*(1), 91–112.

Walters, W. (2012). *Governmentality: Critical encounters.* London: Routledge.

Wodak, R., & Meyer, M. (Eds.). (2009). *Methods of critical discourse analysis* (2nd ed.). Los Angeles, CA: SAGE Publications Ltd.

Wright, W. (1977). *Six guns and society: A structural study of the western.* Berkeley: University of California Press.

Index

Printed in the United States
by Baker & Taylor Publisher Services

Printed in the United States
by Baker & Taylor Publisher Services